101 Things For Kids To Do On A Rainy Day

DAWN ISAAC

PHOTOGRAPHY BY RACHEL WARNE

Kyle Books

For Karen – the best of best friends.

First published in Great Britain in 2015 by
Kyle Books, an imprint of Kyle Cathie Ltd
192–198 Vauxhall Bridge Road
London SW1V 1DX
general.enquiries@kylebooks.com
www.kylebooks.com

10 9 8 7 6 5 4 3 2 1

ISBN 978 0 85783 307 5

Project Editor: Tara O'Sullivan
Editorial Assistant: Amberley Lowis
Copy Editor: Liz Lemal
Designer: Louise Leffler
Photographer: Rachel Warne
Illustrator: Sarah Leuzzi

Production: Lisa Pinnell

A Cataloguing in Publication record for this title is available from the
British Library.

Colour reproduction by ALTA London
Printed and bound in China by C&C Offset Printing Co., Ltd.

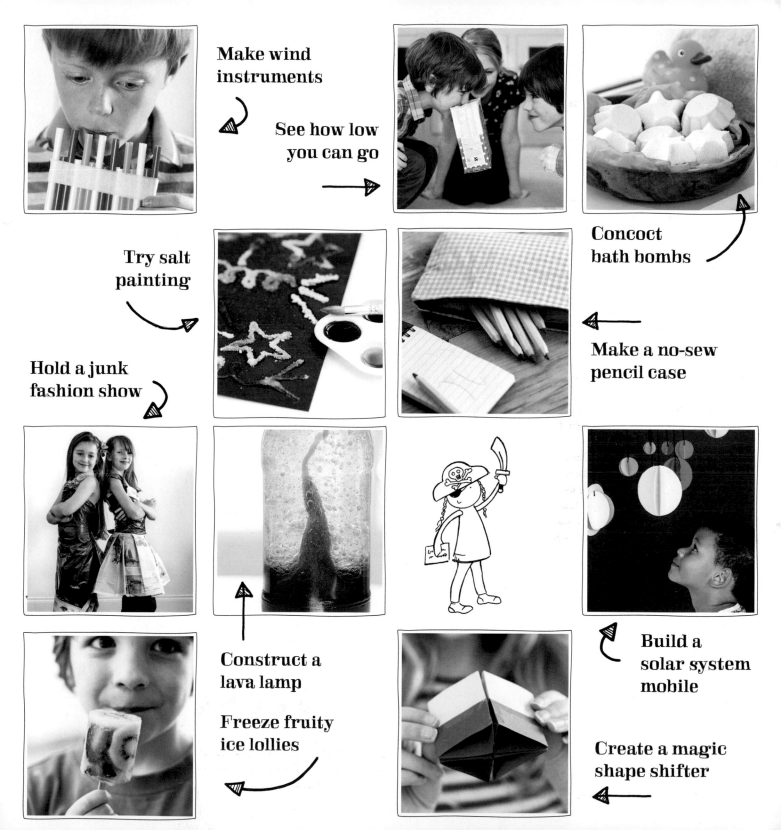

Make wind instruments

See how low you can go

Concoct bath bombs

Try salt painting

Make a no-sew pencil case

Hold a junk fashion show

Construct a lava lamp

Build a solar system mobile

Freeze fruity ice lollies

Create a magic shape shifter

Contents

51. Freeze fruity ice lollies
52. Create a magic shape shifter
53. Make a heart garland
54. Draw optical illusions
55. Grow a garden from scraps
56. Catapult marshmallows
57. Make wind instruments
58. Design your own board game
59. Make an organiser
60. Hold a butter-making race
61. Hold an indoor treasure hunt
62. Make corner bookmarks
63. Wrap a yarn tin vase
64. Make fifteens
65. Prepare a fruity melon bowl
66. Booby trap your bedroom
67. Play flap the fish
68. Create a word search
69. Construct a lava lamp
70. Prepare fresh strawberry tiramisu
71. Fold an origami fortune-teller
72. Build a marble run
73. Set up an indoor obstacle course
74. Launch a Magnus glider
75. Build a solar system mobile
76. Make a no-sew pencil case
77. Create pinwheel sandwiches
78. Play shadow charades
79. Create silhouette portraits
80. Make rainbow fruit kebabs

81. Play the glasses
82. Craft with papier-mâché
83. Run your own library
84. Erupt a volcano
85. Learn a magic trick
86. Decorate a tablecloth
87. Create a jellyfish in a bottle
88. Play wink murder
89. Give your room a view
90. Plant a terrarium
91. Try salt painting
92. Fold a mini book
93. Make string block prints
94. Master 3D drawing
95. Play sticky note scramble
96. Make egg-shaped sculptures
97. Make a severed finger box
98. Catapult a paper plane
99. Set up a juice bar
100. Roll paper beads
101. Have a backwards day

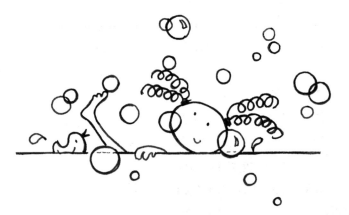

About this book

Sadly, there are days where you simply can't get outside to play: when rain has caused a small river to form outside your house, you have a six-foot snowdrift blocking the front door, a heatwave is making people spontaneously combust or you've had a truly disastrous haircut that you can't risk anyone seeing.

Yes, on these days, even I might think it's okay to stay inside.

But... and I know I'm going to shock you here... that doesn't mean you have to turn on a screen.

In fact, children, gather round, and let me tell you an incredible story. Long, long ago, when dinosaurs roamed the Earth and your parents were kids themselves, people didn't have smartphones, tablet computers, an app for everything or 20 million TV channels.

And do you know the truly amazing part of this tale? They still had FUN!

I know. Unbelievable, isn't it?

Just to prove I'm not making this up, I have gathered together 101 of these mystical 'screen-free' activities. So off you go. What are you waiting for?

There are mummies to wrap, green gloop to make, fingerprints to lift, scrap gardens to grow and volcanoes to erupt.

And when you've finished, if it's still raining or your hair hasn't grown back, I might even have time to tell you another amazing tale. How about 'when fast food didn't exist' or 'the time before plastic'?

I know! Crazy but true!

Play 'Who am I?'

This is a guessing game. And no, it does not involve guessing your own name. I mean, I'm hoping you know the answer to that, otherwise I am going to get seriously worried about you.

No, this involves guessing other people's names.

There are two ways to play. The first involves all players sitting in a circle facing each other. Everyone secretly writes the name of someone famous on a piece of paper before passing it face-down to the person on their left. When you have your piece of paper you hold it on your forehead, facing outwards but without looking at it yourself.

Now begins the guessing. Each player, in turn, asks a question about their person, for example, 'Am I fictional?' or 'Am I male?'. If the answer is 'Yes' you can ask another question and keep going until you get a 'No', at which point the next player gets a turn. The first person to guess correctly wins.

The other version involves working in teams, so needs at least four people to play. Cut or fold and tear some paper so you have lots of small blank rectangles to write on. Everyone gets the same number of 'blanks' each (perhaps 15–30) and secretly writes names of well-known people or characters before folding these over so the others can't see. When everyone's finished, these are all put into a bag and shaken well.

YOU WILL NEED: PAPER, PENS OR PENCILS, BAG, TIMER (FOR SECOND VERSION)

When the other team sets the timer for 1 minute and yells 'Go' the clue giver pulls out one piece of paper at a time and tries to describe the person until their fellow team members can guess the name. And before you get clever, no you can't say 'It begins with D,' or 'It sounds like Javid Heckham'. That's cheating!

Each round a different person has a go at pulling out the pieces of paper and being the clue-giver.

After all the names have been guessed, the team with the most right answers wins.

Tip: If you want to make it a little easier you can give each team one free 'pass' for each round, which they can use if a name proves particularly tricky.

Tip: If you want bath bombs with a twist, you can even add a little plastic gift at the centre that will magically appear as the bath bomb fizzes away.

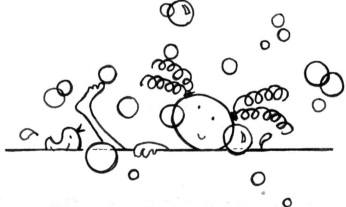

Concoct bath bombs

YOU WILL NEED (FOR 2 BATH BOMBS):
90G BICARBONATE OF SODA, BOWL, FOOD COLOURING, ESSENTIAL OIL (E.G. LAVENDER), TABLESPOON, 30G CITRIC ACID, SPRAY BOTTLE, WATER, SILICONE CUPCAKE MOULDS (OR SIMILAR), BOX OR TISSUE PAPER (OPTIONAL)

I would like to make it clear that these are NOT real bombs. That would be very messy and dangerous, and could seriously put children off washing. There are already enough of you who moan about that – we really shouldn't make it worse.

No, these are fizzing, scented creations that make your bath smell delicious – even when you've spent all day rolling around in mud. Oh, and they also make fantastic gifts, which are great to get you out of trouble – for example, when you've spent all day rolling around in mud...

First, put the bicarbonate of soda in a bowl and add a few drops of food colouring (remember, we are going for subtlety here – not trying to dye you blue), plus a couple of drops of essential oil. Use the back of your tablespoon to squish these as you stir them because they don't spread easily. Now, add the citric acid and mix all the ingredients well.

So, here comes the tricky bit: the bicarbonate of soda and citric acid react with each other in water and fizz like crazy. However, the only way to get your bombs to stick together is to add... water. Yep. You've spotted the problem.

The solution is a spray bottle. Use this, one squirt at a time, to add a fine mist of water to the mixture and then stir as quickly as possible. Keep doing this until the mixture looks like fine breadcrumbs – four to five sprays are usually about right. At this stage you can pack the mixture into a soft case (silicone cupcake moulds work well) pressing it down firmly with the back of your spoon.

The bombs will have dried hard in about 45 minutes and you can then turn them out. They can be a little bit powdery so it's a good idea to present them in a nice box or wrap them in tissue paper. When you're ready to use them, just place a bomb in the bath and watch it fizz like crazy.

Create crossword cards

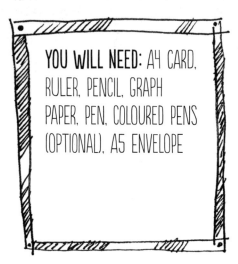

In terms of effort, a card is very much a one-way thing. You design it, make it, write in it – and all anyone else has to do is open it. Don't you think it's about time they worked a little harder?

So, rather than just send a card, why not design a personalised crossword puzzle as well?

First, fold your A4 card in half and then, using a ruler and faint pencil lines, mark out a grid on the front. Using centimetres, you can create one that is 15cm x 21cm.

Use a piece of graph paper to start designing your crossword but make sure it takes up a grid no bigger than 13cm x 19cm so there is a margin when you transfer it to the card.

You could list lots of words about the person's favourite subject, film or book. It's good to start with quite a long word. Write this on graph paper, going across, and then try to find another word from your list that shares a common letter with the first. Write this going downwards, making sure that it crosses the first word at the shared letter.

Keep adding words from your list in this way, both across and down, until you have built up a mini crossword. Transfer these words to the correct positions on the front of your card – again in faint pencil. When you're happy they're right, go over all the lines around the letters in a pen before rubbing out your pencil marks.

Next, number the 'starting' square for each word, beginning in the upper left corner of the puzzle and working your way across and then down. Put a small number in pen in the top left of that individual square starting with '1', then '2' and so on.

Finally, on the left-hand side of the open card, you need to write clues to the answers. Have one list titled 'Across' with all horizontal clues and one list titled 'Down' for the vertical clues. On the other side you can leave space to write your message (which you could always hide in a word search – see page 144–145 – if you really want to make them work hard). When you're done, pop the card in the envelope, ready to deliver.

Tip: For a brighter look, use coloured card or fill in the unused squares of the grid in different colours.

Mix up a dip fest

A plate of raw vegetables is very healthy but it's not exactly... hmm... what's the word... exciting?

So the next time some well-meaning grown-up presents you with this kind of snack plate, you might want to create a few dips to liven it up.

These dips look great served in small dishes or brightly coloured bowls. And if you don't use them all up straight away, they'll keep in an airtight container in the fridge for up to three days. Yes, that's a whole 72 'slightly-more-interesting-than-just-raw-vegetables' hours for you to enjoy.

Simple guacamole dip

YOU WILL NEED:

½ avocado	1 ripe tomato
¼ lime	Garlic leaf
2 teaspoons mayonnaise	Salt and pepper to taste

Mash the avocado flesh using the back of a fork until it's nice and smooth. Next, take your section of lime and squeeze it into the mixture (removing any pips) and stir this in, along with the mayonnaise. Ask a grown-up to cut the tomato in half, then use a teaspoon to scrape the pulp and pips. Add them to your dip along with a snipped up garlic leaf (see pages 118–119). Finally, taste and add a little salt and pepper if needed.

Cucumber and mint dip

YOU WILL NEED:

¼ cucumber	50g cream cheese
2–3 mint leaves	25g natural yogurt

Grate the cucumber using a rotary grater if you can, or a box grater (with a grown-up to supervise). Don't bother to grate the last small section, because it's difficult to do this without also grating your fingers (not a good idea). Then, rip the mint leaves into small pieces and mix these and your cucumber thoroughly with the cream cheese and yogurt before serving.

Soured cream and chive dip

YOU WILL NEED:

50g soured cream	1 chive
10g double cream	½ garlic leaf
¼ lemon	

Mix together the soured cream and double cream. Now, ask a grown-up to cut you a quarter lemon wedge and squeeze this into the mixture (removing any pips which might escape). Use clean scissors to snip up a chive and half a garlic leaf (see pages 118–119). Mix everything together and serve.

Play balloon stomp

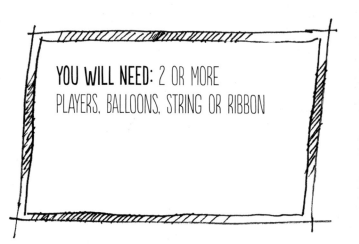

POP!!

You've got to feel a bit sorry for balloons. One minute they're the centre of attention at the party, the next they're just scattered around the floor getting under everyone's feet. So why not give them a second chance at having fun?

First, decide where you are going to play the game. It's best in a room where you can clear a bit of space and also one that isn't filled with a lot of breakables. Balloon stomp is not what you'd call a 'delicate activity'.

YOU WILL NEED: 2 OR MORE PLAYERS, BALLOONS, STRING OR RIBBON

You'll need to have an inflated balloon for each player. Attach a piece of string (or ribbon, which is slightly more comfortable) to the neck of the balloon and then tie this onto your ankle. On 'Go' the aim is to burst everyone else's balloons but to keep yours intact.

The winner will be the last one left with their balloon still inflated.

The only rule is you can't grab or hold onto another person. In fact, as far as possible, this should be a 'non-contact' game. Except for the balloons of course. Poor balloons. I'm starting to feel sorry for them again.

Eek!

Tip: To make the game last longer, tie a balloon to each ankle.

Grow an eggcup micro garden

Grown-ups are no good at understanding sizes. For example, every time they try to get you to eat another weird vegetable they always say:

'How do you know you don't like it? Just try a little bit!'

And then they plonk a huge great chunk of it on your plate. That is NOT a little bit.

Well, here is your answer – grow your very own micro garden and teach the grown-ups in your life what 'a little bit' actually looks like.

First, you'll need some clean empty eggshells with the majority of the shell still intact.

Fill them with cotton wool and wet this well before placing each eggshell into an eggcup on a sunny windowsill.

You can now sprinkle on a few seeds into your egg 'gardens' – a different type for each. Good ones to try are: broccoli, beetroot, Swiss chard, rocket, fennel, coriander, cabbage, spinach, mustard, sorrel, chicory, pak choi, dill and mizuna.

In a few days you'll see the seeds germinate, which means they start into growth by sending out a root, quickly followed by a shoot. Best of all, as soon as this shoot produces its first leaves you are ready to harvest (usually one to three weeks after sowing the seeds).

Just take a clean pair of scissors and snip off the leaves. You can now try a proper 'little bit' of each crop. Be warned though: you might actually like it.

YOU WILL NEED: EGGSHELLS, COTTON WOOL, WATER, EGGCUPS, SEEDS, SCISSORS

Tip: You must never let the cotton wool dry out, so keep a small jug on the windowsill and water whenever you need.

Make a play dough ice-cream parlour

Tip: If you wrap your play dough in a plastic bag after you've finished playing and store it in the fridge it will keep for a week or two.

Until someone actually does the decent thing and buys you your own ice-cream parlour (seriously, how many times can you write something on a birthday list and have it ignored?), this makes a very good substitute. Except for the lack of real ice cream, of course. Apologies for that.

You'll need to make your play dough first. Measure out the water in a jug, add your chosen colour and food flavour extract and stir it well. Now, mix together your salt and flour in a bowl before tipping in the water.

Stir everything with a spoon and when it's beginning to stick together, start to knead it in the bowl. Do this by squashing the mixture flat with the palm of your hand before folding over a side and squashing it again. Keep turning it a little bit each time you do this so you're folding over a different section of the dough.

When it's forming a nice ball, tip it out onto a table that has flour scattered over it and carry on kneading for 10 minutes. This is quite hard work, so feel free to find an idle grown-up and delegate the work to them – they are often just standing around chatting or reading a magazine, and quite frankly, they could do with the exercise.

Now that your dough is ready, you can get creative. The 'ice cream' looks great in sundae bowls but, if you haven't got any, you could use cupcake cases, small bowls, or even make your own cones. To do this, draw waffle patterns on a piece of light brown card then roll it into a cone shape, secure it with sticky tape and trim any extra card off the top.

Finally, finish off with toppings and decorations such as colourful straws, beads or home dyed rice (see pages 102–103).

Just remember: this ice cream is for playing with, not eating (again, I apologise for this enormous failing – but if you do get peckish, look at pages 36–37 to find out how to make real ice cream).

YOU WILL NEED: JUG, 110ML WATER, FOOD COLOURING, FOOD FLAVOUR EXTRACT, SUCH AS VANILLA, PEPPERMINT, ETC. (THIS IS JUST FOR SCENT!), BOWL, 40G SALT, 200G FLOUR, SPOON, BOWLS OR CUPCAKE CASES, LIGHT BROWN CARD, DARK BROWN FELT-TIP PEN, STICKY TAPE, STRAWS AND BEADS

Wrap the mummy

Let's be clear, I said wrap *the* mummy, not *a* mummy. Please don't start dragging unsuspecting women inside your house and coating them in loo roll – that is going to end very badly for everyone.

Instead, you can play this as a game with your friends or family (and yes, this could include a mummy – just make sure you know her).

Players pair up – you can decide who is the 'wrapper' whichever way you want: youngest gets wrapped, roll a dice and highest is the 'mummy', play 'first to 100 in rock, scissors, paper'... it's up to you.

Everyone stands behind a line at one end of a room, then each wrapper gets a roll of toilet paper, and on 'Go' they have to wrap their mummy in it. Legs are wrapped together as one but arms should be separate to the body. Oh, and every bit of the person should be covered – except the eyes, nose and mouth.

You will soon discover that toilet paper rips rather easily. If you want to make the game harder you can make a rule that every time it rips, that wrapper has to start again. Otherwise, just tie pieces together or overlap and carry on.

When the whole toilet roll is used up and a mummy is judged to be covered, they have to hop across the room to a finishing line. Again, if you want to make it tougher, falling over can lead to disqualification (and banning from all pyramids for life... or afterlife).

YOU WILL NEED: 4 PLAYERS (MINIMUM), 1 TOILET ROLL PER TEAM, MASKING TAPE OR STRING (TO MARK FINISH LINE), DICE (OPTIONAL)

Tip: Make sure you do not use the last toilet roll in the house for this game, otherwise you might have a very angry mummy (the real kind).

Pom-poms tied
together make
a soft and fluffy
garland.

Use pom-poms
to decorate hair
bands, clips or
even flip-flops.

Craft pom-poms

Ah, pom-poms: so soft, so squeezable and so cheerful you can almost forgive them for having such a silly name.

To make the perfect pom-pom you need some card discs. If you don't have card to hand you can recycle old greetings cards or cereal boxes instead.

First, draw an outer circle the size you want your final pom-pom to be, using a cup or something similar. Then, draw a smaller circle in the middle of this and about half the size (use an eggcup or coin).

Cut around the larger circle, fold this in half and put a small snip in the middle. When you fold this open the slit will be twice as long and give you enough space to start cutting out the small centre circle (see diagram).

When you have your disc, draw around it on another piece of card and cut out a matching one.

Place the discs on top of each other and begin wrapping them with wool, passing it through the middle each time. Use a piece of wool about four times longer than your arm and hold the ends together so you are threading a double thickness of wool each go, which will cover the discs quicker.

When you have run out of wool, simply cut the same length again and carry on, but make sure you start by wrapping over the end of the last wool length to keep it in place.

When you have coated the discs several times over and the hole in the middle is barely there, tuck the last end of wool under other threads to stop it unravelling.

Now, on the outer edge, push a section of wool to one side, slip scissors between the two discs and start cutting the thread. Once you have cut it all, slip a length of wool between the two discs, bring this all the way round and tie a double knot as tightly as possible to keep your cut wool in place.

Finally, slip off or cut off the card discs and you will be left with a perfect, fluffy pom-pom.

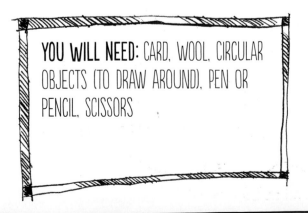

YOU WILL NEED: CARD, WOOL, CIRCULAR OBJECTS (TO DRAW AROUND), PEN OR PENCIL, SCISSORS

Make a card disc

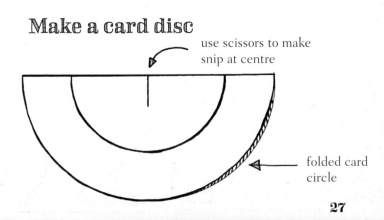

use scissors to make snip at centre

folded card circle

27

Weave a multi-braided bracelet

YOU WILL NEED: CARD, GLASS OR MUG, PENCIL, SCISSORS, STICKY TACK OR PLASTICINE, WOOL

These can also be called 'friendship' bracelets, but why limit yourself? I mean, there's no reason they can't also be 'get-in-your-good-books' bracelets, 'please-forgive-me-for-the-mess-I-just-made' bracelets or even 'don't-forget-my-birthday-is-coming-up-soon' bracelets.

To make any of these bracelets, first create a braiding loom by drawing around a glass or mug on a piece of card. Cut this out and fold it in half one way and then the other so you can locate the centre point. Push a sharp pencil through the centre into a piece of sticky tack or plasticine beneath and twist it around until you have made a good-sized hole.

Use scissors to cut slits along the edge of the cardboard circle where the creases have formed, each one about 1cm deep. Next, add another slit in between each of these pairs so you have eight slits in total.

Take seven strands of wool, each about 40cm long, and tie them together in a knot at one end. Poke this knot down through the central hole in your braiding loom and then spread out the seven strands above so each one is held in one of the slits with only the top slit left free.

Take the strand on the bottom right and move it over to place it in the top slit before turning the braiding loom round so the empty bottom-right hand slit is now at the top. Keep repeating this movement again and again and you will see that a multi-braided bracelet starts to appear through the bottom of your loom.

When the bracelet is long enough, take it off the loom and tie a knot where the braiding ends and then another knot about 2cm further up. You can now snip off any excess wool so you have a neat 1cm tassel at both ends. Finally, slip the beginning of the bracelet through the gap between the two knots at the other end to hold it in place.

Tip: You can use seven different coloured strands of wool but it can also look quite effective to use just two or three colours for a bracelet.

Help!

Tip: For an even stronger colour you can mix a quarter teaspoon of citric acid into the lemonade – just make sure you stir it well until it's completely dissolved.

Pour colour-changing drinks

This is a great trick to freak out your friends and family, plus you can have lots of fizzy drinks because they will ask you to show them this trick again and again. And if that's not enough to make you love science, I don't know what will.

First, you need to make some coloured cabbage water. Rip up a couple of red cabbage leaves into small pieces, put these in a bowl and ask a grown-up to pour on some boiling water so the leaves are just covered. Leave it to cool for 20 minutes, then drain off the juice by pouring it through a sieve into another bowl.

Next, put the liquid into a clear jug and stir in a level teaspoon of bicarbonate of soda – this should make the liquid a bright blue colour. If it still looks a little purple, add more bicarbonate of soda and stir again. Finally, place it in the fridge to chill for half an hour or so.

Now, to freak out your friends...

All you need to do is pour them some lemonade into a clear glass before offering to top it up with your 'magic colour changer'. Now, with as much dramatic flair as you can muster, pour just a very small amount of your blue liquid into the fizzy drink and watch it turn... pinky purple!

If you want to reveal to them how it works, explain that the cabbage has a special pigment in it (an anthocyanin) that changes colour depending on how acid or alkaline something is. Bicarbonate of soda makes the mixture alkaline – and blue – but the acidity in the lemon-based drink turns it pink.

Then again, you could explain nothing... and keep freaking them out. That sounds like a much better plan if you ask me.

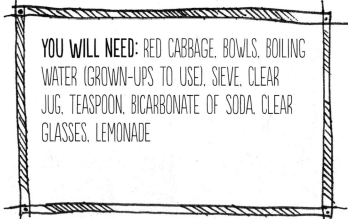

YOU WILL NEED: RED CABBAGE, BOWLS, BOILING WATER (GROWN-UPS TO USE), SIEVE, CLEAR JUG, TEASPOON, BICARBONATE OF SODA, CLEAR GLASSES, LEMONADE

Hold a junk fashion show

Tip: If there are several of you designing outfits, you could give yourself a set amount of time before competing against each other in a vote for the best runway creation.

Move over, Armani, shove up, Chanel, get over yourself, Gucci – there's a new designer label in town. That's right. You can out-couture the best names in fashion and all you're going to need is the odd bin bag and a quick raid of the recycling bin.

You could design an outfit for yourself but it can be easier to dress a model (or in this case, an unsuspecting friend or relative). Good, thick bin bags make a great base for your creation, not least because they are black – always a safe fashion choice. Obviously, you must never put a bag over anyone's head, so either put in large holes for head or arms, or simply cut the whole bag down the side and bottom seam and use it as if it was a flat piece of material.

Masking tape is a great replacement for stitches to hold your costume's shape or to attach other black bin bag material or newspaper sections.

If you want to add straps, why not fold a long length of newspaper over many times to make a strong length of 'material'? Also, pleating newspaper at one end gives a fantastic flared shape that could be used to form skirts, bustles or elaborate necklines.

You can add embellishments by taping or stapling on extra details made from newspaper or even other items from the recycling bin, such as bottle tops or card. And don't forget, you can also create accessories such as hats or bags.

Finally, make sure you have a runway to walk down for your final show, so the editor of *Vogue* (AKA your pet dog) can be suitably impressed by your genius creations.

It's divine
darling!

Hold a dress-up race

If you think getting dressed is a bit dull, then you're obviously doing it wrong. All you need to liven it up is some healthy competition, a bit of time pressure or some dice.

First of all, it's probably best if you put on some underwear before we begin – I don't think anyone needs to see a 'put on your pants' race.

Dress-up dice

Each player lays out their selection of clothes and takes it in turn to roll the dice. You need a '6' before you can start – this allows you to put on a shirt or T-shirt – then it's simply a case of rolling all the other numbers to complete the outfit:

5 – skirt or trousers

4 – jumper

3 – each individual sock and glove

2 – a shoe (but you must have a sock on first)

1 – either hat or scarf

6 – needed to begin the game (shirt/T-shirt) but also for the coat (must go on after the jumper).

The winner is the first person fully dressed.

YOU WILL NEED: LOTS OF CLOTHES, TIMER, DICE

Dress against the clock

Begin with a big pile of clothes in the middle – if you are all different sizes you'll need to put in several items for each person. Jumble them up so people find it harder to spot their own things. Also, make sure you add lots of accessories – hats, scarves, gloves, bags – but nothing too precious or delicate.

On 'Go', set a timer and everyone has 60 seconds to put on as many items of clothing as they can. Things have to be worn correctly: for example, a pair of trousers can't be thrown around your neck like a scarf. And no, I don't believe this is 'how everyone's wearing them these days'.

After a minute everyone has to stop and slowly take off their items to see who was wearing the most.

Warning: Once you have shown that you can put on not just one but several outfits in a matter of seconds, you might be expected to get ready for school a little bit quicker in the mornings.

The third pair of gloves might have been a mistake...

Conjure up ice cream in a bag

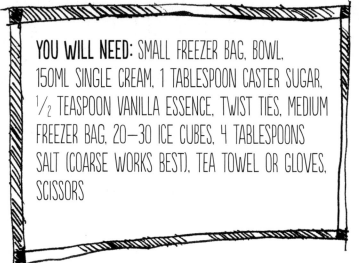

YOU WILL NEED: SMALL FREEZER BAG, BOWL, 150ML SINGLE CREAM, 1 TABLESPOON CASTER SUGAR, 1/2 TEASPOON VANILLA ESSENCE, TWIST TIES, MEDIUM FREEZER BAG, 20–30 ICE CUBES, 4 TABLESPOONS SALT (COARSE WORKS BEST), TEA TOWEL OR GLOVES, SCISSORS

That's right – you can make your own ice cream in a bag and it only takes a few minutes. I know! Why hasn't anybody mentioned it before? This is BIG news.

First, place your smaller plastic bag in a bowl (to keep it from falling over) and pour in the double cream before adding the sugar and vanilla essence. Now – and this is VERY important – squeeze out the air and seal up the bag tightly. You could tie a knot in it or use twist ties – just make sure it's not going to come undone by accident.

Next, place this smaller bag inside the larger one and fill around it with ice cubes – 20 to 30 should be enough – before adding the salt and sealing the outer bag.

Here comes the 'sciencey bit' to impress grown-ups. The salt has the effect of lowering the freezing point of the ice. As it does this, the salty water that forms is so cold it can actually freeze the ice cream. Of course, that means it's also pretty chilly to hold, so you are best wrapping it in a tea towel or putting on gloves and gently shaking the bag (this mixes up the cream and makes sure it all freezes).

After about 5 minutes you can have a feel (through the bag) to see if the ice cream is solid enough. If not, keep shaking for a little longer until it is.

When it feels ready, undo the larger bag and remove the smaller one before running it under the cold water tap to get rid of any salty water on the outside (not surprisingly, salt ice cream has never been a popular flavour).

Now, cut off a corner of the small bag and squeeze your ice cream into a bowl, grab a spoon and tuck in.

Tip: You can also spice up your ice cream by adding some extra ingredients at the start – chocolate chips, chopped strawberries, a few drops of food colouring – it's up to you.

Tip: Always get a grown-up to help set up fairy lights and don't forget to turn them off when you leave the room.

Pitch an indoor camp

Camping is really good fun – except when it's freezing cold, or your tent blows away, or you have to trudge to the toilet block in the middle of the night, or it's pouring with rain and the canopy springs a leak.

In fact, come to think of it, wouldn't it just be easier to camp... indoors?

If you have a small pop-up tent you could use this, but it's much more fun to create your own sleeping quarters. Mops and brooms can be used to make the front entranceway – just tie them together at the top with string.

The back of a chair makes the rear of your tent and when you tie a broom handle or cane to this and the entranceway it forms a top pole.

You can use large sheets or duvet covers to drape over the structure and give you sides and a back to the tent. Tuck these in around the brooms, mops and chair, or use clothes pegs to keep them in place.

Now, why not get comfy? You could bring in your sleeping bags if you have any or just lots of blankets, pillows and cushions.

String fairy lights around the room or even the entranceway itself and you can pretend these are stars lighting the night. Alternatively, you could stick 'glow in the dark' stars around the room or make some of your own from white paper or silver foil.

If you have a torch, place this in the centre of some stones or blocks, prop up sticks – or even painted kitchen roll tubes – around it, add a little red or orange tissue paper and you've made your own mock camp fire.

You now have the perfect spot for reading books by torchlight, playing cards by the fire or scaring each other senseless with your favourite ghost stories. Just make sure you remind any grown-ups around that camping isn't camping without a flask of hot chocolate and some marshmallows.

39

Teach yourself a card game

There are two things you need to know about card games. First, they are addictively good fun and second, they almost always have really stupid names. Seriously – Briscola, Fan Tan, Pitty Pat. Who makes these things up?

Here are a couple of the best (games, not names, that is).

Draw the well dry (2 players)

All the cards are dealt, face-down. The non-dealer turns over their first card and places it in the centre, face-up, followed by the dealer. The game continues like this until one player turns up a 'penalty card' (a picture card, such as a Jack, Queen or King, or an ace).

The other player now has to turn over this number of cards – one card for a jack, two for queens, three for kings and four for aces. BUT if the other player turns over a picture card or ace when paying the original penalty, this new penalty trumps the first and must be paid. Only when a penalty is fully paid can the last penalty card player take the cards. The eventual aim is to win all the cards in the pack.

Fish (3–6 players)

Each player is dealt five cards with the rest of the pack placed face-down in the middle. The player to the dealer's left starts and play continues clockwise.

The aim is to build sets of four cards with the same value – for example, four jacks or four threes.

When it's your go, you can ask any other player for cards to match any in your hand. For example, you could ask 'Ava, do you have any fives?'. If she has one or more fives, she has to pass them over. If not, she replies 'Go fish!' and you take a card from the middle pile to add to your hand. If, by chance, this card is the type you were looking for – in this case five – show it to the group and you get another turn.

Whenever you collect four of a kind, lay these face-up on the table in front of you.

The hand ends when a player gets rid of all their cards. At this point you tot up the scores with one point awarded for each set of four of a kind. You can then shuffle the cards and deal again. The game ends when one player reaches 11 points and is declared the winner.

Tip: Try to remember who has asked for which cards before – this means they definitely have at least one of these.

YOU WILL NEED:
PACK OF CARDS

Set up a school

If you're not always a fan of school, that's okay, because I know you're going to love this one. Why? Well you're running it so, of course, it's going to be brilliant.

You can create a mobile classroom by removing the top, bottom and one side of a large box to leave you with a three-walled structure (you may need a grown-up to help with this – we can call them the school caretaker if you like).

Use some of the leftover cardboard to construct a classroom clock. Draw around a plate to make the circle and then draw a rectangle coming down from this to act as the base (see the photo).

Cut it out and paint on the face and numbers before making two clock hands – one shorter, one longer – from black card. Poke a sharp pencil or pen through the middle of the clock face into an eraser below and do the same to the bottoms of your clock hands. Using a split pin, attach these onto the clock, pushing the 'legs' of the pin apart at the back. Finally, stick the clock base to the back of your classroom with duct tape or staples, so the clock face rises above the wall.

You can also make your own whiteboard. Measure a piece of thick white card just smaller than a clear ziplock bag, then place it in the bag and seal it. You can now use duct tape or staples to attach this to your classroom wall as well as some smaller ziplock bags to hold classroom supplies such as whiteboard markers, registers and, of course, stickers. It is a well-known fact that schools cannot be run without the use of stickers.

You will, of course, need some pupils. If your brothers or sisters don't feel like being taught – or getting expelled – you can always recruit toys. They are much more obedient.

And finally, remember you can teach anything you like – maths, reading, the art of burping on demand. It's up to you. As I said – you're going to love this school.

YOU WILL NEED: LARGE CARDBOARD BOX, SCISSORS, PLATE, PAINT, PAINTBRUSH, BLACK CARD, SHARP PENCIL, ERASER OR LUMP OF PLASTICINE, SPLIT PIN, DUCT TAPE, STAPLER, WHITE CARD, ZIPLOCK BAGS, WALLPAPER/WRAPPING PAPER

Remodel your bedroom

Rearranging your bedroom might sound a great idea, but after you've changed your mind for the fifth time about where to put the bed, your parents might be less enthusiastic.

To develop your interior design skills – and make grown-ups less grumpy – why not start with a plan instead?

Begin by drawing the rough shape of your room on a piece of paper. Now, get your tape measure (it helps to have someone to hold the other end) and find out the length of all of your walls before writing down these figures on your rough plan.

Next, you need to plot this onto your graph paper plan. Obviously, you haven't got a piece of paper as large as your room, so instead you are going to 'scale it down' to 1 in 20. This means that 1cm on your plan represents 20cm in your room and 5cm on your plan is the same as one metre. For example, this means if your room was 3m x 4m, you would draw your room plan 15cm across (3 x 5) and 20cm down (4 x 5).

You can also plot on things like windows and doors by measuring where they are in the room and draw them on to scale. So if a doorway is 80cm across, that would equal 4cm on your plan (because 1cm on your plan = 20cm).

Once you've plotted on everything that can't move, such as windows, doors and built-in furniture, take another piece of graph paper and draw on anything that can move, such as beds, drawers, desks, bedside tables and wardrobes. Again, make sure you measure how wide and long they are and then draw them to scale. Finally, label each one and cut them out.

Put sticky tack on the back of each one and begin by placing everything just as it currently sits in your room – this helps you double-check everything is the right scale. Now you can begin moving things around and working out which arrangement looks best, without straining anyone's muscles in the process.

Bedroom plan

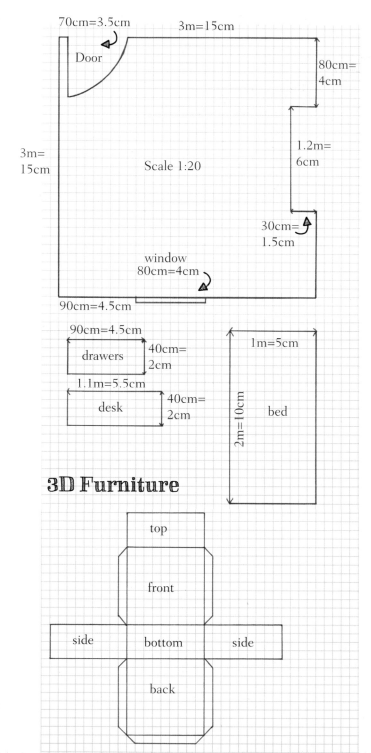

70cm=3.5cm

3m=15cm

Door

80cm=4cm

3m=15cm

Scale 1:20

1.2m=6cm

30cm=1.5cm

window
80cm=4cm

90cm=4.5cm

90cm=4.5cm

drawers

40cm=2cm

1.1m=5.5cm

desk

40cm=2cm

1m=5cm

2m=10cm

bed

3D Furniture

top

front

side | bottom | side

back

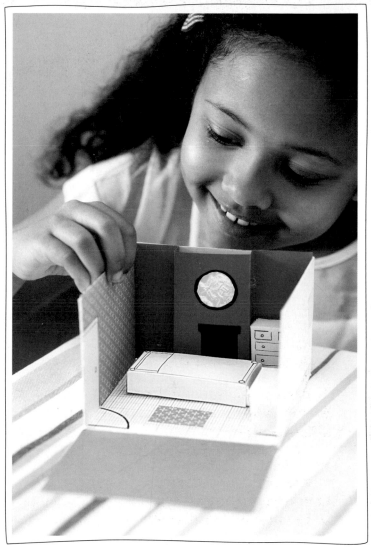

Tip: If you measure how tall your room is, you can draw each wall to scale on a separate piece of graph paper, cut these out and attach everything to thick card joined by masking tape to make a 3D model.

Compete in hands-free ping pong

No hands, no bats, no net and almost no rules – this is ping pong for rebels!

First, you'll need a good-sized table – ideally rectangular but you could make it work on a square, or even round table, if you want. What do we care? We're REBELS!

Put a line down the middle to divide the two playing halves. Masking tape works well as it's pretty easy to peel off afterwards (I mean, I know we're rebels but no one wants to get told off for messing up the table, do they?).

Hands-free ping pong can be played with two people, but teams of two – or more – make it a little easier, and save your breath.

A ping-pong ball is placed at the centre of the middle line and on 'Go' everyone tries to blow it over the edge of the opponent's side. You can defend your own half of the table with your body, but your hands must be behind your back at all times.

A ball over the edge of the opponent's half of the table wins you a point – and the first to five can claim victory.

Tip: To make it messier – and therefore more fun – you can make
all the players eat a dry cracker just before the game begins.
The losing team gets to clean up.

Learn some dice games

YOU WILL NEED:
DICE, PAPER, PENS

Yes, it might not sound promising, but throwing a few numbered cubes around is actually very entertaining. No, really – it is.

Hmm. You still don't look convinced. Why not try these and then see where you stand?

Pig dice (2 or more players)

This is a game of nerves where you have to decide whether to 'bank' your points or take a risk to get a higher score.

Each player rolls in turn. They add together the scores from each throw in that round until they decide to bank them. At this point play passes to the next player. However, if they roll a one before they bank their score all their points on that round are lost. The winner is the first person to bank 100 points in total.

You can also play with two dice. In this version a single one will still lose you all your points from that round but double ones will give you 25 points. Any other double throws will give you double those points – for example, a double four would count as 16 points rather than eight.

Beetle (2 or more players)

In this game players have a piece of paper and pen and must draw a full beetle to win. They take it in turns to roll the dice and add the elements of the beetle as the corresponding number appears:

6 – body

5 – head

4 – wings (need 2 in total)

3 – legs (need 6 in total)

2 – antennae (need 2 in total)

1 – eyes (need 2 in total)

The catch is you have to build the picture in the right order. So you need a six to start as everything builds from the body. Likewise, you must have a head in place before you add eyes or antennae – otherwise you have a page of floating body parts and that's just disturbing.

The winner is the first one to draw a complete beetle.

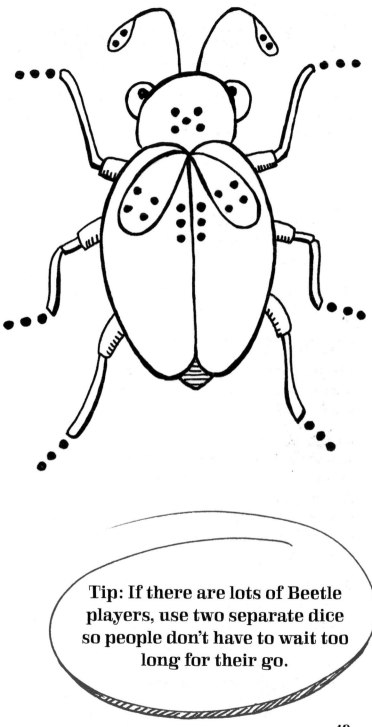

Tip: If there are lots of Beetle players, use two separate dice so people don't have to wait too long for their go.

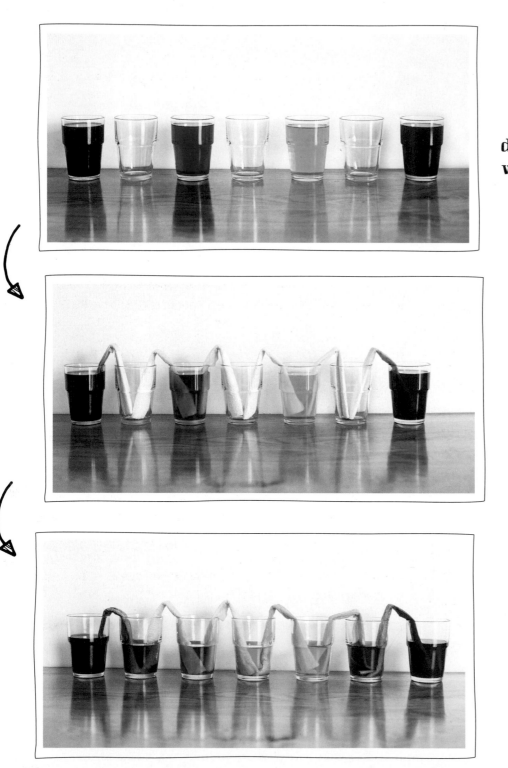

Tip: If you don't have enough glasses, you can do this experiment with fewer colours and either three or five glasses instead.

Watch water walk

We know that water can move by itself. After all, how else does it end up over the floor and walls whenever you have a bath? Exactly!

Still, if grown-ups are sceptical about this you can prove how tricky water can be with this simple experiment.

First, take seven glasses, place them in a line and make sure the first glass is filled with water nearly to the top, and do the same with alternating glasses. This will mean there is always an empty glass sandwiched between two full glasses.

Now, add a different food colouring to each glass of water, starting with red, then yellow, then blue and finally red again.

Take six sheets of kitchen paper and fold each one over several times to make a long, thin shape. Bend each of these in half and place one end in a full glass, the other in the empty glass next door. Repeat this with all the glasses so there are two ends of kitchen paper bent into each empty glass.

And now you can watch and wait... or go and have a bath, whatever takes your fancy. After a few minutes you will start to see each paper towel becoming soaked in coloured water and eventually this water will begin to move out of the full glasses and into the empty ones. At the same time, the colours will also mix to form orange, green and purple water.

If this doesn't convince your parents that water really can get anywhere, then nothing will.

YOU WILL NEED: GLASSES, WATER, FOOD COLOURING, KITCHEN PAPER

Construct a toy parachute

Grown-ups aren't very creative, are they? I mean, if you pass one of them a bin liner, do you know what they'll do? Fill it with rubbish! I mean – how dull is that? Especially when they could be making parachutes instead.

To give a plastic bin liner a much more exciting life, cut down the side and bottom to make a flat sheet. Now, take a ruler and pencil and measure 40cm from the bottom at three different points and join up the line. Do the same from the side until you have marked a 40cm square, which you can then cut out.

Measure and cut four pieces of string, each 50cm long, and use sticky tape to attach them to each corner of your plastic square. Finally, tie the four pieces of string to a small object – toy figures work well but anything that adds a little weight to the bottom of the parachute will do.

Wrap the strings and then the parachute itself loosely around your central object and throw it up into the air – the chute should unfurl as it goes up and then gently float back to the ground.

YOU WILL NEED: PLASTIC BIN LINER OR PLASTIC CARRIER BAG, SCISSORS, RULER, PENCIL, STRING, STICKY TAPE, SMALL TOY OR OBJECT, PERMANENT MARKERS (OPTIONAL)

Tip: Use permanent markers to decorate your parachute.

Make your own jigsaw

You can make jigsaw puzzles out of old greetings cards, pictures from magazines or your own genius artistic creations.

Begin by making your cardboard base. Old cereal packets work well but are a little thin, so it's best to stick two pieces together, with the plain card on the outside. When you do this, make sure you paste the entire surface with a layer of PVA glue by brushing side to side and up and down to get a good covering.

Now paste another thin layer of glue all over the back of your picture and stick this to your double layer of card, smoothing it out carefully as you go. Place this between some plain paper and heavy books and leave it for at least half an hour to stick and flatten out.

Cut out a piece of sticky-backed plastic a little taller than your puzzle and just over twice the width. Unpeel half of it and stick it to the back of your jigsaw, smoothing it out carefully with your hands. Take off the rest of the backing and smooth the other half of the sticky-backed plastic to the front of your puzzle.

Trim any excess covering from the edges of the puzzle and you're ready to create your pieces. It's incredibly difficult to cut tabs for interlocking pieces, so instead use scissors to create shapes which can be pushed together. You can use straight or wavy lines or a mixture of both. You could even add some 'whimsy' pieces for a bit of fun – perhaps the outline of your initial, or a simple shape like a heart, star or arrow.

Just remember, these puzzles are pretty tricky, so don't cut too many pieces (15–20 is good, 250 might be excessive).

When you're finished, have a go at solving the puzzle yourself (you'll be surprised by how tricky this can be).

Finally, place all the pieces in a small box or a ziplock bag to keep them together, ready for the next time you do the puzzle.

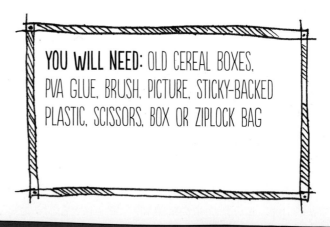

YOU WILL NEED: OLD CEREAL BOXES, PVA GLUE, BRUSH, PICTURE, STICKY-BACKED PLASTIC, SCISSORS, BOX OR ZIPLOCK BAG

Tip: If you can, create or cut out a picture with a border as this will help you find the edges when you come to solve the puzzle.

Tip: If you find it hard to cut out your puzzle, try it with a single thickness of card instead.

Construct a card tower

YOU WILL NEED:
PACK OF CARDS, BUCKET LOADS OF PATIENCE

This is a very simple idea, and yet almost completely impossible and likely to drive you mad with frustration. There – I bet you can't wait to try it now!

First, find somewhere to build your tower. Don't start it off on a slippery surface – something like a carpet or rug, or even a towel laid flat, works much better.

Now, take two cards and place them in an upside down 'V' shape or apex – it can help to use your finger to make sure the cards are lined up well at the top. Once you have this constructed, build another one by the side and then, if this survives, you can carefully place a card across the top of both to bridge this gap. Next, with very steady hands, you can try to build another apex above the first two to give you a second storey.

As you get better, you can add more cards to the lower levels to enable you to build higher storeys and challenge yourself to go three, four or even five storeys tall.

If you haven't already worked it out, this sort of tower is best built away from pets, annoying younger brothers and sisters, slamming doors, draughty windows – oh, and it also helps if you don't breathe on it. Not too tricky at all then...

Tip: Avoid brand new cards (too slippery) and very old cards (usually too bent and creased).

Learn to finger knit

YOU WILL NEED: WOOL, FINGERS

This activity will be very popular with grown-ups because fingers which are knitting cannot be doing other things – like sneaking biscuits, marking walls or picking noses. That fact alone should make them happy to provide you with a ball or two of wool.

First, take the end of your wool and tie it around the thumb on your left hand (or your right hand if you are left-handed). Now, with the palm of your hand facing you, weave the wool around your fingers at their base by going in front of the first, behind the second, and in front of the third. Next, take it behind your little finger and round to the front again and weave back along the row, this time taking the wool the opposite way.

When you reach the end of the row, weave another row to your little finger and back, but this time along your knuckle line. Then, hold the end of the wool by trapping it with your thumb and carefully lift the base stitch on your first finger over the knuckle stitch and off the top of your finger so that it goes behind your hand. Do this with the other three stitches.

Push the line of stitches at your knuckles down to the base of your fingers and then weave another row at the knuckles and carry on.

As you 'knit' more rows of stitches, you will start to see a small scarf appearing behind your hand. You can keep on knitting until this is the length you want.

Finally, you need to finish off. When you have only a single line of stitches at the base, take the loop on your little finger and move it to your third finger on the knuckle. Now, lift the stitch at the base of the third finger over this knuckle stitch and off the top. Lift the stitch from the third finger onto the knuckle of the second and again lift the base stitch over the top. Repeat this until you are left with a single stitch. Cut off the wool, leaving a length of about 8cm, thread this through the final loop and pull it tight.

Tip: If you don't want any gaps between stitches on the finished finger knitting use a chunky wool.

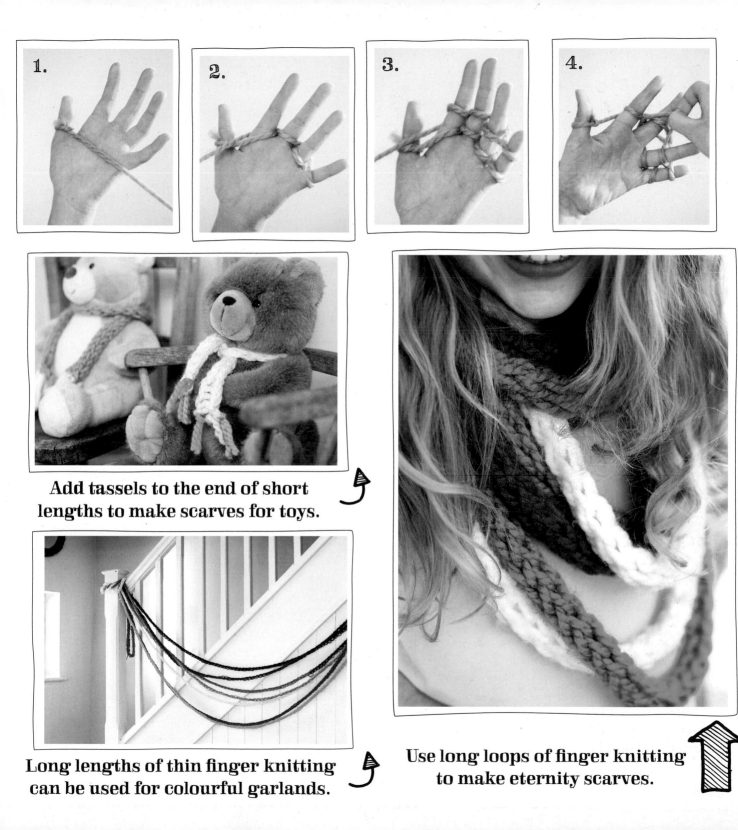

1.

2.

3.

4.

Add tassels to the end of short lengths to make scarves for toys.

Long lengths of thin finger knitting can be used for colourful garlands.

Use long loops of finger knitting to make eternity scarves.

Play patience

If you're stuck on your own with nothing to do, a pack of cards could be a useful friend. Don't get me wrong, they're pretty appalling at sports, don't have any conversation and never invite you for a sleepover. But overlook all of these and you'll realise a pack of cards makes very good company.

Accordion patience

Shuffle your cards and deal them out one at a time. The idea is to end up with as few piles as possible and you do this by moving cards, or piles of cards, on top of each other as you go. You can move cards to their immediate left or three spaces to their left, but you can only move cards to sit on top of a card of the same rank or suit – for example, a six of hearts could be placed on any other heart or the six of spades, clubs or diamonds.

If you run out of space, you can add rows underneath. It pays to think one or two moves ahead to check you are reducing your card numbers as far as possible. The ultimate aim is to end up with a single pile, but be warned – this is extremely difficult to achieve.

YOU WILL NEED:
PACK OF CARDS,
TIME TO KILL

Clock patience

Shuffle your cards and deal them all out face-down in a circular pattern of 12 piles to form your 'clock face', with a thirteenth pile in the centre. Now, take the bottom card from your central pile and turn it over. This card will need putting on the appropriate pile face-up. For example, an ace will go on the one o'clock position, twos on two o'clock etc, with jacks acting as eleven o'clock, queens as twelve o'clock and kings going on the central pile.

Whichever pile is added to, you then take the bottom card from this, turn it over and again add it face-up to the appropriate location. The aim is to turn over all the cards and have them all in the correct positions of the clock – which is harder than it sounds!

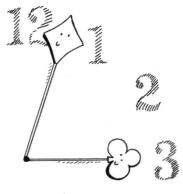

Tip: Keep a pack of cards in the car or your favourite backpack so you'll never be without a friend!

Fashion some spoon dolls

YOU WILL NEED: WOODEN SPOONS, PAINTS, PAINTBRUSHES, PENS, PIPE CLEANERS OR LOLLIPOP STICKS, PAPER, FELT OR MATERIAL SCRAPS, SCISSORS, WOOL, RIBBONS, SEQUINS, ETC., DOUBLE-SIDED STICKY TAPE, NEEDLE AND THREAD (OPTIONAL)

Creating gorgeous dolls is, of course, the best thing you could ever do with a wooden spoon. Unfortunately, grown-ups have a tendency to use them for far more boring things like stirring food, so you'd best check with them before you begin your creation.

It's a good idea to put a base coat of skin colour on the doll first, but if you want to skip this step that's fine – spoon dolls can carry off the natural wood look very well too.

Once the paint has dried you can draw on the face – a thin paintbrush or felt-tip pen is a good plan and can add some colour to the eyes, cheeks and lips.

Make arms by twisting around a pipe cleaner or tying or gluing on a lollipop stick.

Clothes are easily made from paper, felt or leftover material scraps. Cut some slits for the arms and secure the back of your outfit with a strip of double-sided sticky tape. You could even sew it together if you're handy with a needle and thread.

Attach 'blingy' accessories, such as ribbons or sequins with more double-sided tape or even add an underskirt made from circles of tissue paper or small scraps of netting.

Hats are best made in two parts from felt, thick material or card. First, cut a circle or oval for a brim and remove a wide central slit – this allows it to go over the top of the spoon. Now, bend over a second piece of card or material and cut out the top of the hat, leaving a little extra space at the bottom. Thread the top of the hat through the slit and stick the extra tabs against the underside of the brim using double-sided tape to keep it in place. You can sew up the edges of the hat or just disguise them by adding a length of ribbon trim.

Tip: Wool makes ideal hair and you can pre-plait a bunch of strands to add pretty styles.

Making a hat

brim with slit for wooden spoon head

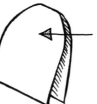

bent over card or material with hat shape cut

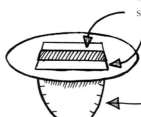

ends of hat stuck down with double-sided sticky tape

hat stitched together at sides (optional)

Create a boredom buster

School holidays, day one: 'No school! Woohoo! This is brilliant! I can do WHATEVER I WANT! Best. Day. Ever.'

School holidays, day two: 'I am SO bored. Why is there never anything to do?'

Thankfully, creating a boredom buster is the perfect activity for the second day of any school holiday.

First, you need a large container of some sort – supersize jars, plastic ice-cream tubs, whatever you have to hand.

Fold an A4 sheet of paper in half lengthways twice and then twice in the other direction so you have 16 rectangles marked. Cut these out and do the same for another four sheets of paper, giving you a whopping total of 80 pieces.

Next, decide on a different activity to write on each. You could begin with ideas from this book, or why not browse through your old toys or games you haven't played in a while?

It's important to get the grown-ups to join in. You should check that they are going to let you do all the activities you are including and also gently suggest that they might want to add the odd treat to the boredom buster such as 'Have an ice cream'.

And if you are wondering how you are going to persuade your parents to allow you to do all of this, here comes the slightly scary part: every boredom buster should include a sense of danger. Yes, you need to sacrifice at least 20 pieces of paper to... chores! These don't need to be huge jobs – 'paint the entire house' or 'do the week's washing' might be going a bit far, but 'vacuum one room in the house' or 'clean a basin' are pretty reasonable.

Now, fold up all your pieces of paper and put them into the boredom buster. For the rest of the holidays if you utter the words 'I'm bored', you can ask to pull out an activity. The only rule is... you have to do it, even if it is 'tidy your bedroom' – so just make sure you really are bored first.

Tip: You can remove any pieces of paper after you have done the activity to stop any repetition, but it can be handy to keep hold of these to add to the boredom buster next holiday.

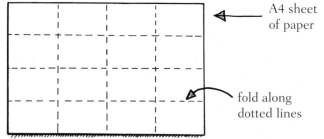

A4 sheet of paper

fold along dotted lines

Take and lift fingerprints

Ever wondered who keeps pinching the last slice of cake? Well, now is your chance to find out.

First, you need to fingerprint all the suspects. Make a fingerprint card for each person with ten spaces: one for each thumb and finger – and label them right thumb, right index finger, right middle finger, right ring finger, right little finger. Then, do the same for the left hand.

If you don't have an inkpad it's easy to make a temporary one. Just take an old plastic container lid and scribble on it with a dark thick felt-tip pen to form a small circle of ink. Now, press down your first suspect's finger on this, rolling it carefully from one side to the other and then, in the correct space on your card, roll the finger again from one side to the other so the print is transferred. Do the same with all their fingers and thumbs. You will need to top up your homemade 'inkpad' as you go.

From this you can work out what features their fingerprints have (see right):

YOU WILL NEED: WHITE CARD, PENS, INKPAD OR FELT-TIP PENS AND PLASTIC LID, ROUND-ENDED KNIFE, WHITE CHALK, BOWL, SOFT BRUSH, STICKY TAPE, BLACK PAPER OR CARD, MAGNIFYING GLASS (OPTIONAL, BUT WHY WOULDN'T YOU?)

Types of fingerprint

Plain arch

Tented arch

Left slant loop

Right slant loop

Plain whorl

Double loop whorl

Central pocket loop whorl

Accidental whorl

Tip: Make-up brushes or soft paintbrushes work well for dusting prints.

Now, you can lift the incriminating print. Take a round-ended knife and use the edge to scrape the end of some white chalk, catching the resulting dust in a bowl. Shake a little of this chalk dust onto the print before using a very soft brush to gently remove all the extra bits.

Carefully cut a piece of sticky tape (making sure you don't touch the middle of the sticky part). Place this onto the print and press it down smoothly. Lift off the tape and attach it to a piece of black paper or card.

Have a good look at the print – using a magnifying glass can help (and will make you look like a top-class detective, which is never a bad thing). Try to spot the key features and see if any of these match one of your suspects' prints.

And if you can't find the guilty party, why not try taking your own fingerprints – and you should probably wipe those cake crumbs off your top while you're at it.

Craft stained glass lanterns

Of course, we're not actually making stained glass – that involves adding metallic salts to molten glass and your parents would probably think that was a teensy bit dangerous. Instead, you can get the look with the help of tissue paper and glue.

First, find a few colours of tissue paper that work well together and cut them into small shapes. You could go for a random pattern or create a specific picture or scene.

Next, coat a section of a clean jar with PVA glue and start to stick on your pieces. Don't worry if they overlap as you go – this just creates a more interesting look.

When you've coated it all, you can paint over the top with another layer of PVA glue, just to make sure everything is well stuck down.

Now, take your length of garden wire, put a loop in one end and start to thread on the beads until you have enough to form a handle. Try to choose beads that go well with the colours of your stained glass.

Wrap the unbeaded section of wire around the neck of the jar and twist it to attach. Undo the looped end and thread this under the wire at the opposite side, pulling it through until just the beaded section is on show. Finally, twist both ends

of the wire tightly and carefully cut off any extra.

Add a little play sand to the bottom of the jar and place in your tea light. The sand keeps the tea light from moving around too much and will also help to put out the flame if it's knocked over.

When it's dark, ask a grown-up to light your tea light so you can see the stained glass colours glow. Oh, and please remember, you should never try to light it yourself because matches can be very dangerous – not quite as bad as melting glass at 1,500 degrees Celsius in your kitchen, but still a safety no-no.

Thread the looped end of the wire under as shown and pull it through until only the beaded section is visible

Tip: You can use a row of stained glass lanterns to provide atmospheric lighting.

Try out hairstyles

Step away from those scissors! This is a no-cut salon – and I think we can all agree that's wise.

Instead, we're going to get experimental with hairstyles, which can easily be corrected if that experiment is a little... unsuccessful.

To create a salon experience, you'll need chairs for customers and a table to hold your mirror and tools of the trade (I saw those scissors sneak in... put them away NOW!).

Place handtowels around your clients' shoulders secured with clothes pegs, and why not have a few magazines around to give them something to read?

Now, armed with hairbrush, clips, grips and bands you can have a go at styling the customer's hair.

If someone has long hair, you could try a top bun. To do this, make your own doughnut bun shape by cutting the end off an old sock and rolling the sock tube in on itself until you are left with a doughnut shape.

Now, put the hair in a high ponytail, thread the doughnut on the end, spread the ends of the hair over it and roll it downwards towards the head, tucking in the hair as you go. At the end, secure it with hairpins.

To add curl to hair, cut strips of material 10cm wide and 30cm long. Wet the hair using a spray bottle or a brush dipped in water and then roll sections of the hair around the middle of each strip before tying the ends together to secure it in place. Leave this until it's dry and then unroll carefully. If you want the curls to stay in longer, leave the 'rags' in overnight.

To make some bright clip-in braids, take three lengths of different coloured wool, fold them in half and knot them all together at the top (leaving a little loop just above to thread your hair clip through). Now, plait the wool nearly to the base before threading on two or three beads and adding a knot below to keep them from falling off.

Make a doughnut bun shape

Make a clip-in braid

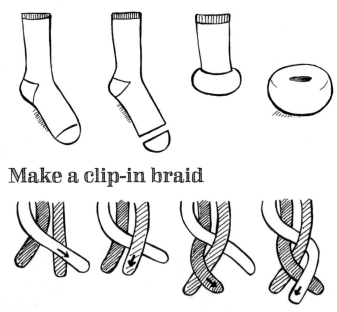

Tip: If you use pinking shears to cut your 'rags' they won't fray too much.

YOU WILL NEED: CHAIRS, TABLE, MIRROR, SMALL TOWELS, CLOTHES PEGS, HAIRBRUSH, HAIR ACCESSORIES, OLD SOCK (FOR BUN), MATERIAL (FOR RAGS), PINKING SHEARS (OPTIONAL), SPRAY BOTTLE (OR BRUSH TO DIP IN WATER), WOOL, BEADS AND HAIRCLIP (FOR BRAIDS)

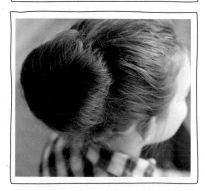

Tip: You could cut out pictures of different hairstyles from magazines to decorate the walls of your salon.

Tip: If you want a really waterproof surface, ask a grown-up if you can paint it with varnish.

Learn to paper patchwork and decoupage

Sticking on some pieces of colourful paper can brighten up boring boxes, personalise picture frames and, best of all, turn pieces of rubbish into perfect gifts. That's right: rubbish + glue + paper = free presents. So what are you waiting for?

First, you need to find some paper, such as tissue paper, bits of wrapping paper or even leftover pieces of wallpaper. Use a few different types, but try to make sure they look good together. Either cut the paper into shapes or rip it into pieces if you want a 'shabby chic' look.

Mix two parts PVA glue with one part water in a bowl. Use the paste to paint a section of whatever object you are covering. You can now begin sticking on your first pieces of paper. Overlap the shapes slightly to get a patchwork look and to make sure every bit of the object is covered.

Or you could try decoupage. This just means 'cutting out pictures', but it's a French word, which makes it sound more impressive. Cut around pictures from old magazines, wallpaper or wrapping paper. Now, just stick these onto the object using the same PVA mixture. If it's already a nice background colour, you could just paste on one or two pieces. Or else you can overlap the cut-outs in the same way as for the patchwork design.

Whichever method you choose, make sure all your pieces are stuck down carefully and then, when the object is dry, paint it all over with a coat of PVA glue – this will dry clear and shiny. You can add several coats of this for more protection; just make sure the glue dries between each coat.

You can use this method to decorate old cans, cardboard boxes, plastic pots, trays, chunky bangles, wooden coat hangers, picture frames and much, much more.

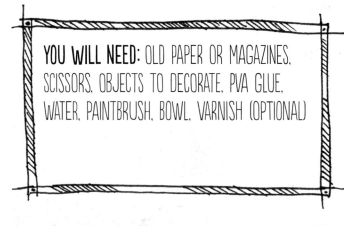

YOU WILL NEED: OLD PAPER OR MAGAZINES, SCISSORS, OBJECTS TO DECORATE, PVA GLUE, WATER, PAINTBRUSH, BOWL, VARNISH (OPTIONAL)

Mix bath paints

Baths are inspiring places. Yes, there's nothing like wallowing around in a sea of bubbles to get your artistic juices flowing. Thankfully, by mixing up a few bath paints, you can let the world see your amazing artwork. Lucky old world, eh?

First, find some small tubs or a paint-mixing tray – just make sure they are plastic so they're safe in the bath. After all, we both know at some point you're going to drop them.

Now, shake up the shaving foam bottle and put a little in each tub or slot.

STOP! I said a little.

Yes, you should have now realised that the foam gets bigger after it first comes out, so maybe next time you could wait and see how much you've squirted before adding more.

Once you have a pile of foam about the size of a small bar of soap in each, you need to add the food colouring. Use a few drops of colour for each swirl of foam and stir these in with a small spoon (use a different spoon for each one or you will muddle up the colours).

At bath time you can use brushes or just your fingers and hands to create your own bathroom gallery on the tiles, the inside of the tub... and probably yourself. Yes, you might be a creative genius but I'm also guessing you're a messy one.

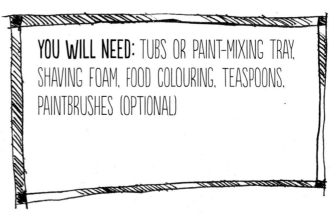

YOU WILL NEED: TUBS OR PAINT-MIXING TRAY, SHAVING FOAM, FOOD COLOURING, TEASPOONS, PAINTBRUSHES (OPTIONAL)

Tip: Ask a grown-up to check the paint to make sure it won't stain the grouting between the tiles.

74

Create your own bingo game

'Legs 11!'

'Knock at the door, number 4!'

'Two little ducks, 22!'

Yes, it's worth making this game just so you can shout weird bingo calls.

Begin by creating your cards. Take an A4 sheet of card, fold it in half, open it out and cut along the fold line to make two cards. Now, use a ruler and pencil to mark 3cm spaces down the sides and across the top and bottom before joining these up with a felt-tip pen to make a grid five squares across and seven squares down.

Label the top row 'B', 'I', 'N', 'G' and 'O' and underneath write the number ranges for each row – '1–10', '11–20', '21–30', '31–40', '41–50'.

If you want permanent cards, you should fill in the spaces selecting numbers at random from the ranges to make cards like the one shown here.

Or save yourself a job – leave the cards blank and ask your players to choose their own numbers

B	I	N	G	O
1-10	11-20	21-30	31-40	41-50
2	11	22	33	43
3	12	23	34	45
4	16	25	37	46
7	17	26	38	47
10	19	30	40	49

YOU WILL NEED:
3 OR MORE PEOPLE, A4 CARD, SCISSORS, RULER, PENCIL, FELT-TIP PEN, HAT OR CONTAINER, SWEETS (HOPEFULLY)

from the ranges above. This means it's more likely you'll have people getting bingo at the same time as they could have picked the same numbers but, as always, it's the first to actually shout out 'Bingo!' that wins – so be alert!

Now, take more pieces of A4 card, mark the 3cm grid as before, but this time cut out the squares. You can give 25 of these to each player so they can cover over their numbers once they've been called out.

Take more squares, number them 1–50 and place them in a hat, bowl or any container you choose. The caller, without looking, will now pull out one at a time and shout out the number (with appropriate bingo call). Any player with that number on their card can cover it over and the first to have a whole line covered shouts 'Bingo!' and is awarded one point. Carry on playing and the first person to cover over all their numbers also calls 'Bingo!' and gets two points.

You could play first to three or first to five.

Tip: Ask a grown-up if you can use sweets as counters to cover numbers and then 'points awarded' can change to 'sweets you are allowed to eat' at the end of the game.

Tip: As well as using traditional bingo calls you could try making up some of your own.

BINGO!

Set up a café

Cafés are great places. Not only do they give you a choice of what to eat, they also, almost always, serve ice cream. Seriously (grown-ups should take note), this is a much more fun way to eat.

If you want to demonstrate this, why not set up your own café? First, you're going to need some tables – smaller side tables are good, but if you're a bit short on those you could just use both ends of a bigger table. Put out clean tea towels as small tablecloths or, if you've got some spare material, you can use pinking shears to create your own (the pinking shears stop the material fraying too badly).

Don't forget to put a number on each table – this means you'll remember which order to take where and also allows you to yell out things like 'Chef, three large strawberry ice creams for the extremely greedy customer on table one, please!'.

Oh yes, and chairs are handy too – customers get a bit funny when you suggest they stand up to eat.

You'll also need to create some menus. First, decide what you're going to offer – you could use plastic food or some you've made yourself from salt dough (see pages 96–97) or play dough (see pages 22–23). Or for the 'wow factor' why not knock up some real dishes (see list on page 216).

YOU WILL NEED: SMALL TABLES AND CHAIRS, TEA TOWELS OR CLOTH (FOR TABLE COVERS), CHAIRS, CARD (FOR MENUS), SMALL NOTEBOOK, PEN/PENCIL, TEA TOWEL AND DRESSING GOWN CORD OR STRING (FOR APRON), FOOD (REAL OR FAKE), TIP JAR (COMPLETELY NECESSARY), CASH TILL (OPTIONAL), EXCELLENT CUSTOMER SERVICE (OPTIONAL BUT WILL HELP SECURE TIPS)

Find a small notebook to take down the customers' orders and, to give you the authentic 'waiter' look, attach a tea towel around your waist with a dressing gown cord or piece of string for an apron.

Oh, and don't forget to remind all your customers when presenting the bill that 'service is not included' and hold the 'tips' jar under their nose. That usually does the trick.

Build a shoebox house

Get off your tiptoes! I know you've grown, so don't worry – this is a house for you to build, not live in. But do make sure you keep growing – especially your feet – because we're going to need shoeboxes.

Start by deciding on the layout of your house. Each shoebox will form a room and it's a good idea to begin with a large one at the base before adding another storey or two. You can use more than one box per floor – just make sure that the structure doesn't topple over.

When you're happy with the look of the house, begin taping together all the boxes. You should connect the front, sides and backs to each other wherever you can. Masking tape is ideal as it's easy to paint over afterwards.

You could add chimneys to the top by using toilet roll inners or other tubes. Cut 2cm slits up from the base all the way around, then press these out to form tabs which you can tape over to keep the chimneys in place. You can also make a sloped roof by cutting the corner off a cereal box and taping it to the top of a shoebox. When the structure is complete, paint the outside and leave it to dry.

You can now unleash your interior design skills. Measure the base of the 'rooms' and cut this size of felt or foam to make carpets. These can be stuck with glue or double-sided sticky tape.

Measure the sides and back of each 'room' before cutting out pieces of wrapping paper to the right size. Now, use glue to paste your 'wallpaper' to the walls.

White paper works well for the ceiling and also as a base for windows. Simply cut out matching pairs of squares, rectangles or circles. Fold these pieces of paper in half and then quarters, before unfolding them and using a thick black pen over the fold lines and edges to make windowpanes. Finally, stick one to the inside of the box and the other in the same place on the outside.

Tip: You can make furniture for your house out of small boxes (matchboxes are ideal) or craft some from salt dough (see pages 96–97).

Have an indoor snowball fight

Snowball fights are brilliant... unless you get a really hard one right in your face of course, or your hands get so cold you can't roll any more, or someone puts a snowball down your back.

Actually, I take it back – snowball fights are rubbish. Except if you have one indoors.

And no, not with real snowballs, in case you were wondering (and please tell me you weren't wondering that or I shall be very worried about you). No, instead you can use pieces of scrunched-up newspaper.

There is nothing to stop you just pelting these at each other in a frenzied attack. But if you want to employ a bit more skill, you can set up a proper fight. First, divide up the room you are playing in – you could put a line of masking tape across the floor or lay down a piece of string. Each player, or team, can only stand in their half of the room and everyone gets the same number of snowballs to start – 10 or 15 work well. These are then placed in a line just back from the centre.

On 'Go', everyone grabs their snowballs and tries to hurl them at their opponents. If you hit anyone they are 'out', but if they catch the snowball, then you're out instead.

As the room may well have some furniture in it, you can always hide behind this. But you must make sure you each have the same amount of 'safe spots' and also, no one is allowed to hide behind these for more than a count of ten.

Which all makes it sound like a very organised game. But really, whichever way you look at it, this is just about pelting each other with newspaper balls... and that's got to be a good thing.

YOU WILL NEED: OLD NEWSPAPERS, MASKING TAPE OR STRING

Tip: If you haven't got old newspaper, you could scrunch up balls of any scrap paper or alternatively, why not make some large colourful pom-poms to use instead (see pages 26–27).

Create a kaleidoscope

Kaleidoscopes use mirrors to make things look amazing – so why not make your own?

Start by cutting three strips of mirror card. For a tube 5cm in diameter, these strips need to be a little over 4cm wide and 1.5cm shorter than the tube itself. Tape the pieces together with the mirrored surfaces pointing inwards to form a triangular prism and push this into your tube so it sits flush with one end – this will be your viewing point.

Trace around the tube end onto a piece of clear plastic (old recycled food containers work well) and also a piece of opaque plastic (such as a plastic milk container). If you can't find opaque plastic, use clear plastic and stick on a circle of greaseproof paper.

Push the clear plastic into the non-viewing end of your tube. If it's a snug fit, it should hold itself in place. If not, use sticky tape to connect it to the sides. On top of this pour in beads to fill two thirds of the space so there's room for them to move around, and then attach your opaque disc over the end of the tube with sticky tape.

Take a piece of card and draw around a circle a little larger than the end of your tube. Now, place your tube in the centre of this circle and draw around it as well. Cut out the larger circle and use scissors to make snips from this outer edge to the inner circle every centimetre to create tabs.

Next, trace around a small coin in the middle of the centre circle and cut this out by folding the card in half and making a small snip in the middle. When you open it up, this slit allows you to get your scissors in and cut from the middle outwards.

Bend down the outer tabs of the circle, place it on the viewing end and tape the tabs to the side of the tube.

Now, hold the tube loosely in one hand and twist it gently with your other while looking through the view hole. You'll see incredible patterns as the beads move and the mirrored prism creates multiple reflections. Tah dah!

YOU WILL NEED: KITCHEN ROLL CARDBOARD TUBE (OR SIMILAR) AT LEAST 5CM DIAMETER, MIRROR CARD, SCISSORS, STICKY TAPE, CLEAR PLASTIC, OPAQUE PLASTIC (OR GREASEPROOF PAPER), PEN, THIN CARD, CLEAR PLASTIC BEADS

Making a kaleidoscope

clear plastic beads

opaque plastic disc

clear plastic disc

tube

mirrored card prism

black card viewing end

See-through plastic beads work best because light can shine through them.

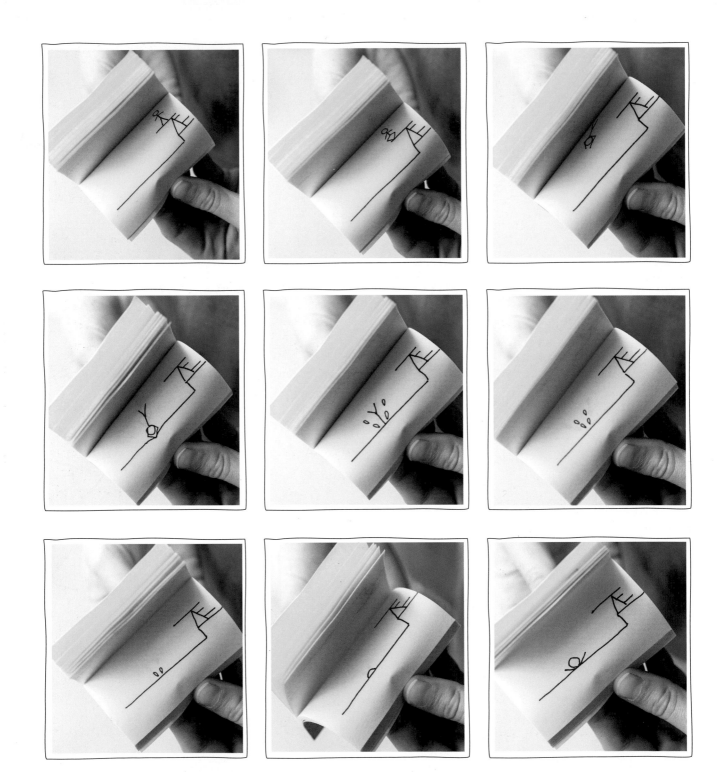

Make a flipbook

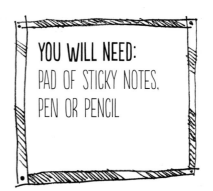

We all know you should be able to make brilliant cartoons – after all, you have spent hours and hours researching them. Well, now's the chance to prove how good your animation skills really are.

Start with a pad of sticky notes. Grown-ups sometimes use these to write boring messages and reminders to themselves, so it's best to check if they can spare you one. In fact, you could just use a corner of each sheet to make your flip book – this way they can still write their boring messages like 'pay the bills' or 'buy cat food', but these are massively improved by having your works of art on them.

Start with the back page of the pad and draw your first picture. Just remember to make it simple because these pads can be a hundred pages long and that's a lot of drawing.

Now, let the next page flip over and check that you can see your original drawing through this. You want to create a feeling of movement, so this second picture should start to show the beginnings of this. For example, if it's a stick man kicking a ball, you might see one of his legs moved back slightly this time. Do the same with the next sheet, again just moving the scene along a bit more. The smaller the change each time, the smoother the cartoon will eventually look.

As you keep going you can check your work by beginning to flick through the book – just lift up the pad with your thumb and let it move up the edges of the pages, releasing them quickly one after the other.

Because your brain is trying to make sense of what it's seeing it will basically fill in the blanks or missing pictures based on what it's already seen – which is very clever... and makes you wonder why grown-ups' brains can't remember to pay bills or buy cat food without it being written down on silly bits of paper.

Tip: Use pale-coloured notes and a dark pen as this will show up best through the sheet above and make it easier to trace on your next 'movement'.

Set up a spa

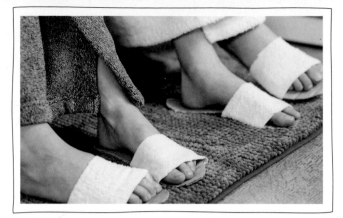

This is worth doing just to sit around in your dressing gown for hours. Yes, I know you do this anyway, but for once you'll have an excuse.

You can also pop on some flip-flops or make spa slippers for the occasion. To do this, trace around your feet onto a piece of thick or corrugated card. Cut out these shapes about half a centimetre out from the line. Get two strips of material 6cm wide and 18cm long – an old towel cut up is ideal, but any thick soft fabric works well. Position this over the widest part of the foot-shaped cardboard and then fix either end to the underside with some duct tape.

If you want to have a pedicure, part-fill a washing-up bowl with warm soapy water and leave your feet to soak for 15 minutes. You can use a small nailbrush to give them a good clean (which will make a nice change for them) before drying them on a towel and rubbing in some moisturiser.

You can have a manicure in a similar way, but this time put the bowl on a table next to you so you can leave your hands to soak there.

And to look really ridiculous why not mix up some face masks?

Chocolate mask

1 tablespoon cocoa powder
4 tablespoons double cream
½ teaspoon honey

Mix the ingredients together to form a smooth paste.

Fruity mask

½ very ripe banana
½ very ripe avocado
½ lime
1 tablespoon natural yogurt
2 tablespoons oatmeal

Mash together the banana and avocado until the mixture is as smooth as you can make it. Squeeze in the lime juice and then stir in the yogurt and oatmeal until well mixed.

When you have made your mask, spread it on so your face is covered (but not the area around your eyes). Leave it on for a maximum of 10 minutes before rinsing off with warm water and patting your face dry.

YOU WILL NEED:
FOR SLIPPERS: CARDBOARD, PENCIL, SCISSORS, SOFT MATERIAL, DUCT TAPE WASHING-UP BOWL, SOAP, NAILBRUSH, TOWEL, MOISTURISER, FACEPACK INGREDIENTS

Tip: To make sure you look appropriately silly, don't forget to place a slice of cucumber on each eye. And no, I've no idea why you do this either.

See how low you can go

The challenge is... to pick up a cereal box from the floor.

What's that you say? Seems a bit easy? Oh, yes, sorry, I forgot to mention, you have to do it using only your mouth.

Still a doddle you say? That's because I failed to tell you about having only your feet on the ground – no kneeling down, no hands out to steady yourself, no elbow supporting allowed.

Hang on – you've all done it ten times already? Silly me. I should have told you that before their go, each player has to tear a strip of card off the top of the packet all the way round. That's right, the packet will get lower to the floor every time. Oh, and the moment you overbalance, put anything other than your feet on the floor, drop the packet, knock it over or pass out through sheer concentration – you're OUT! There – now it's a challenge!

Tip: To make it harder, you can get each player to pick up the packet and place it on a table or do the whole thing while balancing on one leg or playing a banjo (actually, even I think that might be going too far).

YOU WILL NEED:
2 PLAYERS (MINIMUM),
EMPTY CEREAL PACKET,
SENSE OF BALANCE,
FLEXIBILITY, NERVES OF
STEEL

Construct a no-sew shoulder bag

You could learn the ancient art of sewing – mastering hemming, conquering the running stitch, wowing people with your ruching. Or you could just get out your stapler and a roll of duct tape. Oh! What a surprise! You went for the second option.

First, fold your large piece of fabric in half before measuring and cutting out a rectangle from each bottom folded corner, 2cm wide and 3cm high.

Open out your fabric and on the back begin adding strips of duct tape all the way across. Each new strip should slightly overlap the last. When the whole back of the fabric is covered, use scissors to trim off any extra tape.

Now, take one of your long strips of fabric and add duct tape along a long edge so that half its width is covering the fabric and then bend it over and stick it down to seal the edge completely. Do the same on the other side before folding in both edges so they meet in the middle. Add a piece of duct tape along the length to join these two sides together. Repeat this with the other piece of fabric for the second strap.

YOU WILL NEED: FABRIC 80CM X 40CM, RULER, SCISSORS, DUCT TAPE, TWO STRIPS OF FABRIC 70CM X 10CM, STAPLER

Making your bag

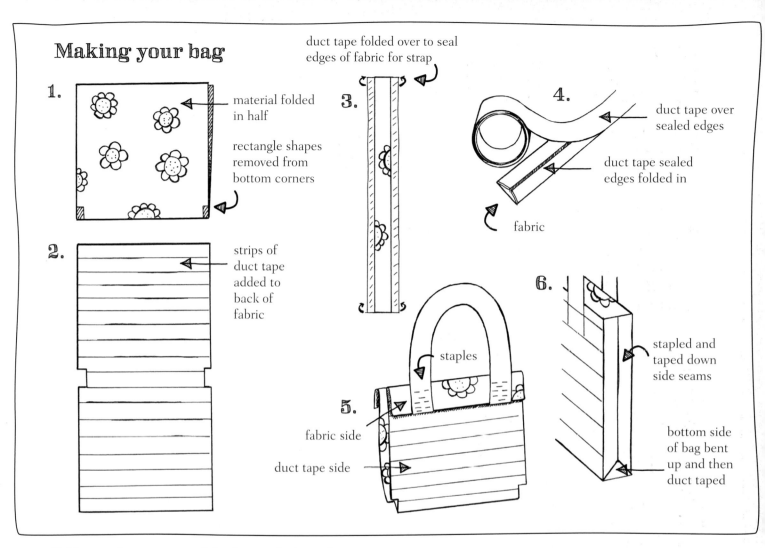

1. material folded in half

rectangle shapes removed from bottom corners

2. strips of duct tape added to back of fabric

3. duct tape folded over to seal edges of fabric for strap

4. duct tape over sealed edges

duct tape sealed edges folded in

fabric

5. staples

fabric side

duct tape side

6. stapled and taped down side seams

bottom side of bag bent up and then duct taped

Fold over the top 6cm of the bag and place the fabric side of each end of the strap against the fabric inside edge of the bag. Decide where you want both straps to sit and then staple the bottom 5cm of each strap to the inside fold using several staples. Cover the staples and hold the top fold in place by adding a couple more strips of duct tape. Now, do the same to the other side.

Put the front and back of the bag together, duct tape facing outwards, and staple up the sides 2cm in from the edge. Press open these seams and stick them down with duct tape.

Stand the bag up and flatten out the bottom and you will see the material at the corners form a triangle shape. Bend these up and duct tape them on top of the side seams.

Finally, turn the bag the right way out and it's ready to be filled with anything you want – perhaps a needle, thread and a 'How to sew' book.

Tip: Thicker fabric works best.

Hunt the thingy

YOU WILL NEED:
A THINGY

This game was traditionally called Hunt the Thimble.

'What is a thimble?' I hear you ask.

Well, it's something used in sewing.

'And what is sewing?' you reply with a puzzled expression.

Hmmm. This is why we might be safer using a thimble replacement – or 'thingy'.

Your thingy should be something small – about 1–2cm tall and roughly the same across. To make the game challenging it's probably best if it's not too bright and obvious – a token from a board game, a bottle top, a dice, that sort of thing.

Now, the searchers leave the room while the hider places the thingy somewhere. The only rule is it must be in plain sight – nobody should need to lift or move anything to be able to find it.

The other players now enter the room and try to find the thingy, while the hider sits in the middle and watches.

'Wow! That sounds really easy!' I hear you shout.

Ah yes, but remember how small it is. Now, combine this with how very bad most children are at finding anything: their coats, toothbrushes, sense of responsibility. See – not so easy after all.

When someone spots the thingy, they must try not to make it too obvious, but instead go and sit down in the middle of the room – probably with a smug expression on their face – where they can whisper its location to the hider. The last person to find the thingy is given the role of hider next time.

Tip: If only two of you are playing the game, take it in turns to be hider and searcher and the winner is the one to locate the thingy in the fastest time on their go.

94

Model with salt dough

YOU WILL NEED: 200G FLOUR, 100G SALT, BOWL, 120ML WATER, JUG, FOOD COLOURING (OPTIONAL), METAL SPOON, COOKIE CUTTERS (OPTIONAL), RIBBON OR STRING (OPTIONAL), ACRYLIC PAINTS AND PAINTBRUSHES (OPTIONAL), TEA LIGHT (OPTIONAL)

As one of the main ingredients is salt, you should have worked out that, unlike cookie dough, this is not a treat to nibble. Try to forgive it, though, because it's very good for making things with – and that's almost as good as eating.

First, mix the flour and salt in a bowl. Now, measure the water in a jug and, if you want coloured dough, add a few drops of food colouring before giving it a stir.

Pour the water bit by bit into the bowl, mixing with a metal spoon as you go. Keep adding it until the dough is moist enough to hold together in a ball when you press it with your hands.

After kneading for about 10 minutes (see pages 22–23) the dough should have a smooth finish and be ready to use.

Hanging ornaments are very simple to make – just roll out your dough to an even thickness and use cookie cutters to form shapes. If you make a hole in the top with a straw, you can thread and hang the ornaments with ribbon when they're dry.

Another easy gift is a tea light holder. Simply create an object or shape – just make sure it's at least 5cm deep and nice and flat on the base. Press in a tea light to the centre and leave it there while the dough starts to air dry. When it's mostly hard, remove the tea light for final drying.

You could even create some salt dough furniture for your shoebox house (see pages 80–81). If you're joining separate pieces – perhaps a tabletop and legs – simply moisten both surfaces with water and then press them firmly together.

You can leave your salt dough creations to air dry on a piece of paper – this will take a couple of days for thin items like the hanging ornaments, but it could take a week for large pieces. Remember to turn them occasionally so all parts can dry properly.

If you're impatient (I can't believe I wrote 'if' there), ask a grown-up to bake them in the oven at 80°C for a couple of hours before letting them cool on a rack.

Tip: You can paint your salt dough when it's dry (unless you coloured it at the start).

Tip: It's best to use salt dough when it's fresh, but if you need to you can store it wrapped in clingfilm in the fridge for up to three days – just remember to knead it on a sprinkled flour surface when it comes out.

Make green gloop

The trouble with green gloop is that to a grown-up's ears, it sounds a bit messy. And to be honest with you, it is a bit messy.

So... here's some advice. Rather than asking 'Can I make green gloop?' just say 'I would like to undertake an experiment with a non-Newtonian fluid to increase my scientific knowledge'.

This will undoubtedly impress your parents so much that they will say yes even though they haven't a clue what you're talking about.

Begin by putting on an apron or some sort of protection for your clothes and place a wipeable cloth or old newspaper on the table.

Add some green food colouring to your water, mix it well, and pour this into a bowl with the cornflour. Slowly stir it with your hands until it combines to form a gloopy mixture – about the consistency of a thick batter. If it's too liquid, just add a little more cornflour, and if it's too thick, add a bit more water.

When your gloop is perfectly gloopy, you can start experimenting with this non-Newtonian fluid. First, try prodding the mixture and you'll find it acts like a solid, but let your fingers just rest on the surface and they'll disappear into what feels like a liquid.

You can also try rolling a handful of it between your palms. The pressure of rolling the ball will keep it in shape. But stop and you can watch as it melts away through your fingers.

And why not lightly punch the gloop and then quickly pull back your fist? You might expect this to send it splattering all over the place but instead the mixture turns hard where it's struck.

This all happens because the tiny bits of cornflour are held in the water – when you stir this around slowly the cornflour and water particles are able to move past each other. However, if you suddenly add pressure, the water moves away more quickly, leaving the particles of cornflour to pack together tightly, forming a solid. There, that's the science bit over with – you can go back to playing with the gloop now.

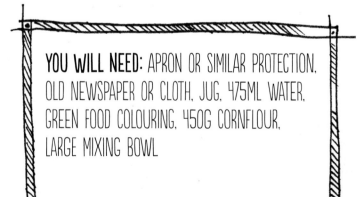

YOU WILL NEED: APRON OR SIMILAR PROTECTION, OLD NEWSPAPER OR CLOTH, JUG, 475ML WATER, GREEN FOOD COLOURING, 450G CORNFLOUR, LARGE MIXING BOWL

Tip: You can add any colour you want to this gloop, but if it's green you can pretend you have just done a really, really messy sneeze.

Race around the world

Yes, it is possible to run from Iceland to Jamaica via Peru without leaving your house. This game can be played with two players but adding more people = more mayhem = more noise = more fun (I like to call this the chaos creation equation).

First, make your journey cards by copying out the ones opposite. These cards give a list of countries and the destinations you can travel to next from each one. If you want to reuse the game, use strong A4 card. You could even laminate it or cover it in sticky-backed plastic.

Next, someone who isn't playing the game needs to hide the eight journey cards all around the house. Make sure they can be seen, but don't make it too easy. Use sticky tack to stick them behind doors, to the sides of baths, even on ceilings, using as many rooms as possible.

Write each starting location (found at the top of the solution lists) on a separate piece of paper, fold these up and let everyone pick one at random. All the players also need a pen or pencil and a passport to keep a record of their journey. This can simply be a folded piece of paper, or you could

make mini books (see pages 192–193).

On 'Go' everyone races around trying to find their first location on one of the hidden journey cards. When they find it, they must note down where they must travel to next and now find the card with this location on it, and so on.

The first one to get 'home' must race back to the referee and have their travel log marked against the solution checklist card. There is only one correct way to complete each journey, so if it matches, they are declared the winner.

Journey Card 1

Portugal ➜ HOME
Chile ➜ Colombia
Philippines ➜ Peru
Oregon ➜ Texas
Kansas ➜ Honduras
Colorado ➜ Paraguay
Guyana ➜ Argentina
Panama ➜ Greenland

Journey Card 2

Georgia ➜ Bhutan
South Africa ➜ Sudan
Honduras ➜ HOME
Oman ➜ Mongolia
Niger ➜ Ethiopia
Cameroon ➜ Libya
Romania ➜ Turkey
Peru ➜ Jamaica

Journey Card 3

Bulgaria ➜ Georgia
China ➜ Canada
Russia ➜ Colorado
Germany ➜ Poland
Ethiopia ➜ HOME
Japan ➜ California
Pakistan ➜ Thailand
Belize ➜ Portugal

Journey Card 4

Thailand ➜ Philippines
South Korea ➜ Kansas
Hawaii ➜ Belize
Bangladesh ➜ Vietnam
Paraguay ➜ Namibia
Sweden ➜ HOME
Texas ➜ Uruguay
Argentina ➜ Kenya

Journey Card 5

Mexico ➜ Guyana
Vietnam ➜ Indonesia
Italy ➜ Pakistan
Greenland ➜ Sweden
Hungary ➜ HOME
Australia ➜ Hawaii
Sudan ➜ Yemen
Bolivia ➜ Zambia

Journey Card 6

Kenya ➜ Oman
Poland ➜ South Korea
Libya ➜ Jordan
Austria ➜ Bulgaria
Turkey ➜ India
Uruguay ➜ South Africa
Jamaica ➜ HOME
New Zealand ➜ Chile

Journey Card 7

Namibia ➜ Cameroon
Bhutan ➜ Malaysia
California ➜ HOME
Yemen ➜ China
Zambia ➜ Chad
Iceland ➜ England
India ➜ Singapore
Indonesia ➜ New Zealand

Journey Card 8

England ➜ Italy
Canada ➜ HOME
Malaysia ➜ Panama
Singapore ➜ Australia
Chad ➜ Germany
Jordan ➜ Hungary
Mongolia ➜ Japan
Colombia ➜ Niger

Solution 1
Start at: **Mexico**

1. Guyana
2. Argentina
3. Kenya
4. Oman
5. Mongolia
6. Japan
7. California
8. Home

Solution 2
Start at: **Iceland**

1. England
2. Italy
3. Pakistan
4. Thailand
5. Philippines
6. Peru
7. Jamaica
8. Home

Solution 3
Start at: **Oregon**

1. Texas
2. Uruguay
3. South Africa
4. Sudan
5. Yemen
6. China
7. Canada
8. Home

Solution 4
Start at: **Bolivia**

1. Zambia
2. Chad
3. Germany
4. Poland
5. South Korea
6. Kansas
7. Honduras
8. Home

Solution 5
Start at: **Romania**

1. Turkey
2. India
3. Singapore
4. Australia
5. Hawaii
6. Belize
7. Portugal
8. Home

Solution 6
Start at: **Bangladesh**

1. Vietnam
2. Indonesia
3. New Zealand
4. Chile
5. Colombia
6. Niger
7. Ethiopia
8. Home

Solution 7
Start at: **Russia**

1. Colorado
2. Paraguay
3. Namibia
4. Cameroon
5. Libya
6. Jordan
7. Hungary
8. Home

Solution 8
Start at: **Austria**

1. Bulgaria
2. Georgia
3. Bhutan
4. Malaysia
5. Panama
6. Greenland
7. Sweden
8. Home

Make an I-spy jar

You know when you tidy up your bedroom or a playroom... No? Okay, imagine *if* you tidied up your bedroom or playroom. You'd be likely to find lots of small bits and bobs lying around – a lonely jigsaw piece, a stray paperclip, the odd counter from a game you don't even remember owning. Well, rather than scratching your head wondering where they all belong, you can use them to make your own I-spy game.

First, you'll need to find a container. Tall thin jars work well, or you could use a clear plastic tube or even a plastic bottle – just make sure it has a lid.

Fill your container almost to the top with rice to get the right amount (using a funnel will help – especially if filling a bottle). Now, empty the rice out and divide it into equal parts: one for each food colouring you have.

Place each portion of rice into a plastic container with a lid or a ziplock plastic bag, add a few drops of food colouring, seal it and shake hard. If the colour isn't strong enough add some more food colouring and keep shaking. Once you are happy the rice is all coloured, you can spread it on some kitchen paper to dry out.

While the rice dries (and this can take some time) start gathering all your items. The main thing is that the pieces are small enough to be well disguised in the jar of rice. Also, make sure you list

YOU WILL NEED: TALL GLASS JAR, CLEAR PLASTIC CONTAINER OR CLEAR PLASTIC BOTTLE WITH LID, FUNNEL (OPTIONAL), RICE, PLASTIC CONTAINERS WITH LIDS OR ZIPLOCK BAGS, FOOD COLOURING, KITCHEN PAPER, SMALL ITEMS, BOWL, PAPER AND PEN OR PENCIL (TO LIST THE ITEMS)

everything you are going to include so players can mark them off when they're found.

Mix all the dried rice with the objects in a bowl before pouring them carefully into the jar (or use the funnel again) and finally, place the lid on. If you want to, you can tape the lid in place to make sure players don't open it.

To play you can take it in turns to see who can spot the most items in a minute or simply pass it between players who all have to spot something new within 20 seconds or they're out of the game.

Tip: For a more subtle look, you could make a game filled with green, red and brown lentils and add in objects that will blend well with the colours, such as nuts, tiny pine cones, old coins or a piece of pasta.

Become a mind reader

With this simple trick you can amaze your friends, surprise your friends, confuse your friends – even make your friends really annoyed when you won't tell them how it works. All in all, it's going to be an emotional rollercoaster for your friends. In fact, you might well lose the odd one by the end of it, but let's not worry about that now...

First, you need an accomplice (maybe choose the friend you don't want to lose).

While you wait outside the door this friend will ask the audience to choose an object in the room. Now, when you re-enter you can ask your friend to begin pointing at objects at random around the room but explain that, through reading their mind, you will be able to identify the 'mystery object' when it's selected.

Of course, both of you need to agree your 'golden rule' before you begin any of this. This rule will be the trick that lets you know when the chosen object is being pointed to. Your friend will point to an agreed *something* first, so that you know

the mystery object will be next. It could be that the object will be whatever your friend points to after pointing at a person, the second thing he or she points to after pointing at something made of wood, or perhaps the thing he or she points to with their left hand, rather than the right – it's up to you. Just make sure you can both remember it.

However convincing your mind reader pose is, your friends will soon realise that there is some trick to this. When you've demonstrated your mind reading a few times you can let them take it in turns to be the 'mind reader' and see if they can work out how it's done by leaving the room but then correctly guessing the object on their return. When one or two have identified the golden rule you can let the others in on the secret and then see if they can come up with their own golden rule to fool the group.

Try to use a suitably 'mystical' voice – this helps set the mood (and irritates people just a little bit).

Craft paper flowers

You can make these flowers in any colour or size, they don't cause hay fever, never need watering and can't die. All in all, it's enough to make real blooms feel rather inadequate.

Ruffle circle flowers

Place eight sheets of tissue paper in a pile and draw around a circle on the top layer – using a mug or small saucer – before cutting out all the sheets in one go.

Fold this stack of circles in half, then quarters, and finally eighths and use scissors to cut one of the shapes below. If you find this difficult because the pile is too thick, just stop folding at quarters and cut the shapes from here instead.

Now unfold and, holding all the[ ]
place their centre over the eras[er]
pencil end through this point ar[ ]
to create a small hole. Thread th[e]
cleaner through and bend and tw[ ]
tissue sheets can't slip off.

Take the top tissue circle and, h[ ]
together, pinch and twist the ba[se]
the sheets below, one by one, u[ ]
your ruffled flower. Finally, put[ ]
pipe cleaner flower stem just [ ]
itself.

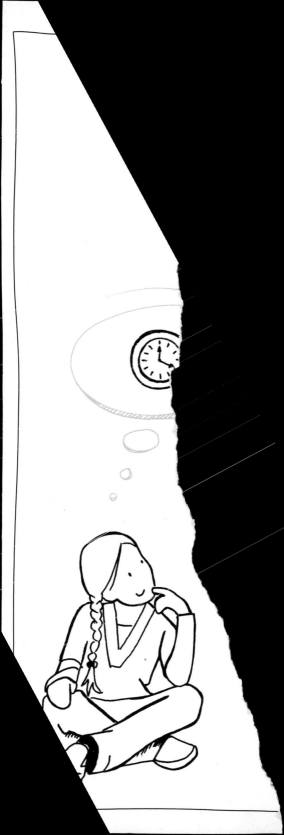

SHARP
GOLF
D)

circles together,
er. Push a sharp
d into the eraser
end of your pipe
ist it over so the

olding the sides
se. Do this with all
til you've created
a twist into the
below the flower

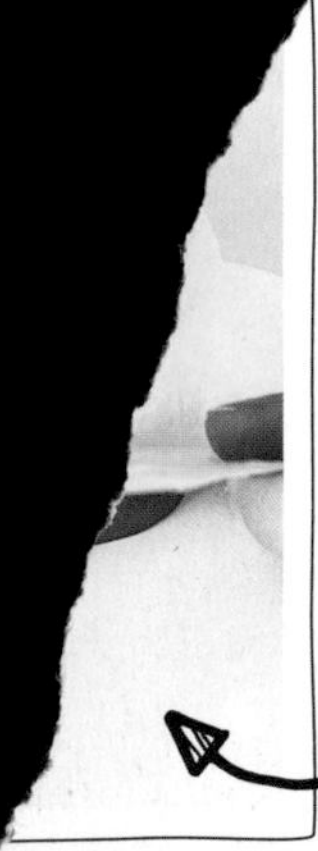

**A sharp
pencil pushed
through the
tissue into an
eraser makes
a hole in the
tissue without
marking your
table.**

Full petal flower

Place five sheets of tissue paper on top of each other and then cut them out in one go to form rectangular shapes 16cm x 8cm.

Now, place a ping-pong or golf ball in the middle of one of the sheets, bring the edges together at either side of the ball and gently twist the paper at both ends until it makes long, thin tapers.

Remove the ball carefully and cut one taper shorter so you have 0.5cm of twist at the end of a puffed out petal. Do this four more times until you have five petals.

Hold the long taper ends together so the petals form a flower shape and then wrap the end of your pipe cleaner tightly around these ends three or four times. Finally, cut off any excess twists hanging below the pipe cleaner swirls.

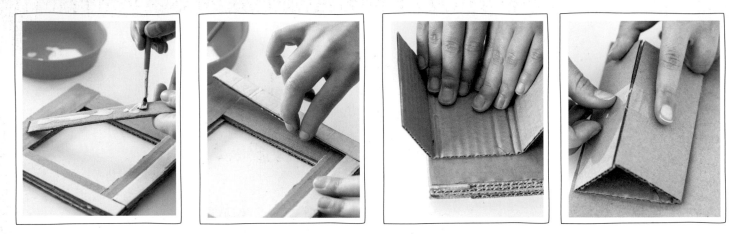

Tip: You can add more decorations to your frame by sticking on small, lightweight objects such as sequins or buttons.

Construct a picture frame

There are so many gorgeous things deserving a proper frame: photographs of you, snaps taken by you, pictures drawn by you. To make sure quality work gets a quality frame, it's probably safest if you use a frame made by you too.

Begin by cutting strips of cardboard 3cm wide (recycled packing boxes work well), then cut these into two different lengths – six pieces 9cm long and another six pieces 15cm long. Finally, cut a strip of cardboard 1.5cm wide and cut this to form two pieces 15cm long and one 12cm long.

On a flat surface, place two of the long 3cm wide strips at the side and use two 9cm strips to connect these top and bottom to form a square. Coat the upper surfaces with PVA glue and lay on another four pieces, but this time with the longer strips at the top and bottom and the shorter strips at the sides. Take the thinner strips and coat the bottom of them with the glue before laying the longer pieces along the sides and the shorter piece along the base.

Paste the top of these strips with glue and place on another four pieces of 3cm wide card, long pieces top and bottom and short along the sides.

Finally, coat the top layer with more PVA glue and lay on a 15cm square of card. Place a book on top to keep the structure weighted down for 30 minutes while the glue dries.

Cut a final piece of cardboard 16cm long and 10cm wide. Mark and fold it at the 12cm and 6cm lines, paste the outside of the middle section with glue and line this up with the bottom of the frame. Weight it down while the glue dries, then use sticky tape to connect the two ends of the cardboard to create a triangular stand for the picture frame.

If you like, you can use decoupage techniques (see pages 72–73) to paste on small pieces of paper around the sides and front of the frame to cover some of the corrugated edging.

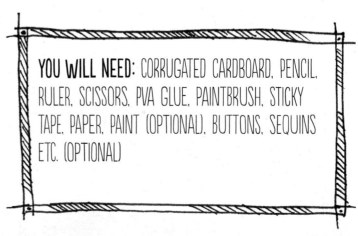

YOU WILL NEED: CORRUGATED CARDBOARD, PENCIL, RULER, SCISSORS, PVA GLUE, PAINTBRUSH, STICKY TAPE, PAPER, PAINT (OPTIONAL), BUTTONS, SEQUINS ETC. (OPTIONAL)

Freeze fruity ice lollies

These lollies are made with fruit juice and fresh fruit so they're actually pretty healthy. But please don't let that put you off.

If you haven't any lolly moulds, it's pretty easy to make your own. Take a clean, dry empty yogurt pot – and no, not a family size one or you'll be licking your lolly for several hours. Instead, choose the little individual ones that hold about 85g.

Turn your pot upside down on a piece of card and draw around the top. Cut this shape out, fold it in half, unfold it, and fold it in half the other way before snipping a 0.5cm cut either side of the middle line so the cuts themselves are only a couple of millimetres apart. Open it up and pull out the middle piece you have snipped.

Cut your fruit into pieces, taking out any pips and green stalks and then place them in the yogurt pot. Just make sure you position some nice looking fruit against the sides. Finally, fill to just below the surface with fruit juice – white grape juice is good because you can see the colour of the fruit through it.

Place your piece of card on top of the pot and carefully insert your lolly stick through the slot you have snipped away. To make sure it holds up straight, you can mould sticky tack around the base. Repeat the process if you're making more than one lolly.

Ask a grown-up to place this in a freezer until it's fully frozen – this usually takes a few hours or you could put it in overnight.

When it's taken out, remove the card and sticky tack and let your lolly stand on a plate for a few minutes (the warmer your house, the less time it needs, so make sure you keep checking). When the edges have softened enough, you can gently twist the lolly out of the pot and begin licking.

Make ice lollies

lolly stick

card with slit cut in

yogurt pot

Tip: Don't worry if you haven't got lots of fruit to hand. Just use fruit juice. It'll still be delicious.

Create a magic shape shifter

There is probably a very important maths and engineering lesson you can learn by creating this shape shifter – something about right-angled triangles or Pythagorean theory, perhaps. But really, the best reason to make it is because people will say 'Wow, that's incredible!'

First, use your ruler to measure a piece of paper 24cm wide and 12cm long and cut it out.

On the shorter sides, make marks at 3cm and 7cm before joining these up so you have two lines running across the the paper. Next, make a mark every 3cm along the top and bottom of the paper and connect these up too, to make eight strips.

Cut out the strips and fold them along both lines and join the ends together with tape to make a right-angled triangle (see, I told you – there's some maths for you right there!). Lay these triangles out on their long sides in two rows, with four on each side and the right angles meeting in the middle.

Take the top two triangles on the left-hand side and tape together their longest sides. Do the same with the bottom left-hand pair and repeat this for the other side.

Next, join together the left-hand pairs by putting a piece of sticky tape between their shortest sides, and repeat this on the right.

Finally, hold the two sides together so you have all their shortest sides showing (this should look like a series of eight squares). Tape together the two bottom squares and the two top squares.

You can now start manipulating your shape shifter. The pieces of tape act as hinges, which means you can bend and change the shape you make with the triangles to form loads of different structures. Which is – that's right – incredible!

Make a shape shifter

1.

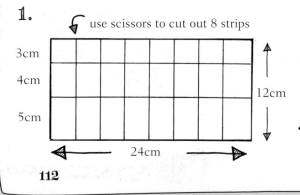

use scissors to cut out 8 strips

3cm
4cm
5cm

12cm

24cm

2. tape sides together to form a triangle

3.

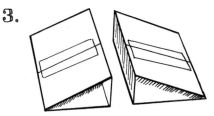

tape triangles together in pairs along longest side

112

Tip: You can use strips from different coloured paper to make a super bright version.

tape pairs together along shortest side

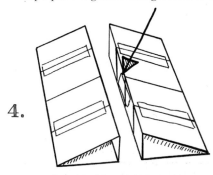

4.

add final pieces of sticky tape to join shortest sides of triangles at either end of shape shifter

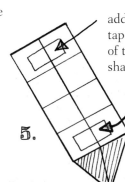

5.

YOU WILL NEED: RULER, PAPER, PENCIL, SCISSORS, STICKY TAPE

Make a heart garland

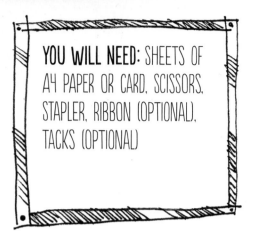
YOU WILL NEED: SHEETS OF A4 PAPER OR CARD, SCISSORS, STAPLER, RIBBON (OPTIONAL), TACKS (OPTIONAL)

Hearts really are the best shape in the world. Not only are they guaranteed to make grown-ups sigh at how thoughtful and sweet you are (and possibly forgive you for all sorts of things), they're also very simple to create.

To make a whole garland of hearts all you need is some paper or thin card, scissors and a stapler.

First, fold your paper or card lengthways and cut along the fold line. Do the same with each of these two pieces and the same again with the four this creates. Eventually, you should have eight long strips.

Take one of these, bend it over so the ends meet and press it flat to form a fold halfway along. Do the same with a second strip. Then, with the first one, bend the two ends in on themselves and you will see a heart shape form. Slip the folded end of the other strip of paper between these two ends so the paper edges line up and staple them all together.

Now you just need to fold the ends of the second strip in on itself to form another heart shape and again slip a folded strip between these and staple.

Keep on repeating these steps until your garland is the length you want. If you are making a circle shape to go over something, you can staple the first heart shape between the last two ends to finish it off or else leave it as a long strip and hook the ends onto something or sticky tack them in place.

If you use card rather than paper you could make longer heart garland strings and use these to form a door screen. Just staple a short length of ribbon between the last heart ends and put a tack through these to attach it to the top of a door frame. Oh, and you should probably warn people you are making a screen or grown-ups might not be sighing and thinking how sweet you are when they accidentally walk into it.

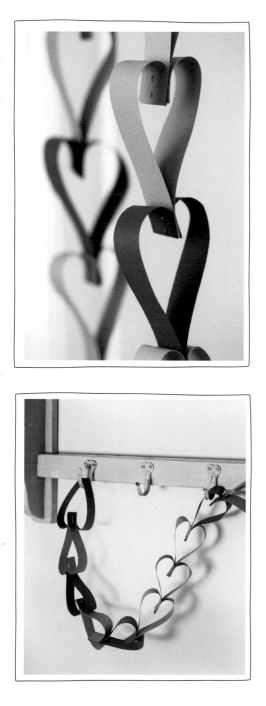

 Tip: You can alternate different colours of card or paper when you make your garland.

Draw optical illusions

Optical illusions almost always have ludicrous names – the Pogondorff illusion, the Muller-Lyer illusion, the Flugenhafentrump illusion. I mean, you couldn't make these up!*

They're also brilliant for tricking the eye and making people go 'No, I don't believe it!' And for once they won't be talking about your homework excuses.

The Pogondorff Illusion

Using a ruler, draw a steep diagonal line halfway down your paper in black felt-tip pen, then finish that line in red. Now, draw another line using your ruler about 1cm above the first, but this time only draw in the bottom half and use a blue felt-tip pen.

Finally, fold your piece of black paper over twice lengthways so it forms a tall black rectangle. Lay this over the centre of your drawing and ask people if they can see which colour the black line leads into. They will think it's the blue one, not the red: the fools!

YOU WILL NEED: PAPER, RULER, BLACK, RED AND BLUE FELT-TIP PENS, BLACK CARD OR PAPER, GRAPH PAPER

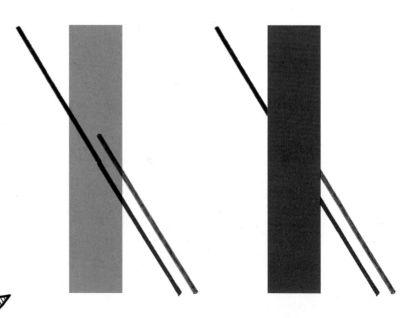

The Muller-Lyer arrow illusion

Draw two lines on a piece of paper, parallel to each other and the same length. To one add outward-facing arrows at both ends and to the other, inward-facing arrows. Ask people which is longer and their eyes will tell them it's the bottom one.

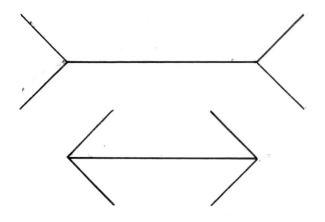

* Actually, that isn't true because I did make up Flugenhafentrump. But you've got to admit, that would be a brilliant name.

Tip: You can draw your illusions in faint pencil lines first before going over them in felt-tip pen, just in case you make a mistake.

Sander's parallelogram

Take your piece of graph or squared paper and draw a line diagonally down in blue felt-tip pen across the squares, lining them up carefully as you go. Do the same in the other direction for the same number of squares, to create a wide 'V' shape. Connect the blue lines at the top with a black felt-tip line.

Also in black, draw in a bottom line the same length as the top line but set in a couple of centimetres (or squares) from the right. Join up the top and bottom black lines at both sides to create a parallelogram. Finally, draw a line parallel to these side lines, joining the point of the blue 'V' to the top line.

Now, ask people which of the blue lines is the longest. It will look as though the left-hand side one is much bigger but you'll know they are both exactly the same length.

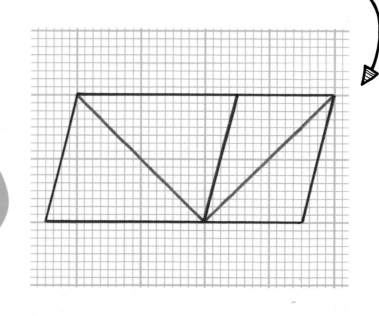

Tip: Remember to keep your scrap garden watered – this is the other essential thing for plants (very much like ice cream is for children...).

Grow a garden from scraps

Grown-ups have a habit of throwing away useful stuff – especially in the kitchen. In fact, almost any time they go near fruit and vegetables something goes to waste. Well, now you can teach them some better habits by showing them how to grow new plants from their scraps.

Find a nice sunny windowsill where you can house your garden – sunshine is completely essential to plants (very much like sweets are to children).

You should then hover over your parents' shoulders every time they are preparing something to eat. They will, of course, find this spectacularly annoying, but that's nothing new.

If they're chopping up celery, ask to keep the bottom section when they have cut it off. Pop this in a shallow dish of water and in a few days it will start to regrow from the centre. Also, if you save the ends of spring onions you can stack these in a small glass, with the roots at the bottom, give them some water, and you'll have more leaves to snip off in a couple of weeks. Plus any cut-off tops of root vegetables like carrots, beetroots, turnips or radishes can be put on a saucer in some water and they will start to regrow.

And when your mum or dad say 'Oh, dear' as they pull out the vegetable basket, that's your cue to grab things. Onions that have started to sprout or garlic cloves past their best can be planted in a pot of stones. Just water up to the base of these 'bulbs' and they'll start producing leaves which will taste of, well, onion and garlic not surprisingly, and which you can snip with scissors to add to your cooking (see pages 16–17).

And don't forget, any leftover seeds and pips from fruit can be put into a small plant pot of compost to see if they'll grow. Just make a hole with your finger, pop in the seed, cover it over with compost and give it a water.

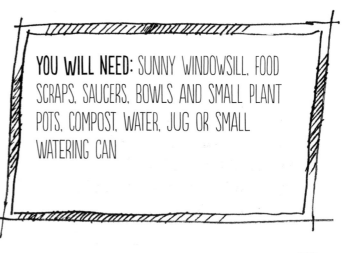

YOU WILL NEED: SUNNY WINDOWSILL, FOOD SCRAPS, SAUCERS, BOWLS AND SMALL PLANT POTS, COMPOST, WATER, JUG OR SMALL WATERING CAN

Catapult marshmallows

So, okay, if we're really honest, you don't have to use marshmallows for this – anything small and light will do. But there is absolutely no reason grown-ups need to know this. Just show them the 'You Will Need' section and then take this book away... quickly.

Once you have your 'large bag of marshmallows' (see how kind I am), it's time to get inventive. The aim is to build the best catapult you can using only lollipop sticks, elastic bands and a plastic spoon.

If you're doing this on your own you can take your time to work out and refine your design, but it adds more excitement if you get at least one other person involved and turn it into a competition.

Agree a set amount of time – maybe 20 minutes – for each player to build their catapult. When the time is up, you need to position yourselves behind a line and each try to fire a marshmallow as far as possible.

You can even make it a competition of three rounds, with each player getting a chance to refine or even rebuild their catapult in the 20 minutes between launches.

Oh, and the winner gets to eat their marshmallows... and maybe everyone else's too. Thank goodness you've got a large bag of them.

Make a catapult

you can use a couple of elastic bands to attach your spoon to a lollipop stick to make your launcher

pull back your launcher against a rubber band and then let go to release the stored energy

triangular shapes are really strong and very useful in building up a catapult shape

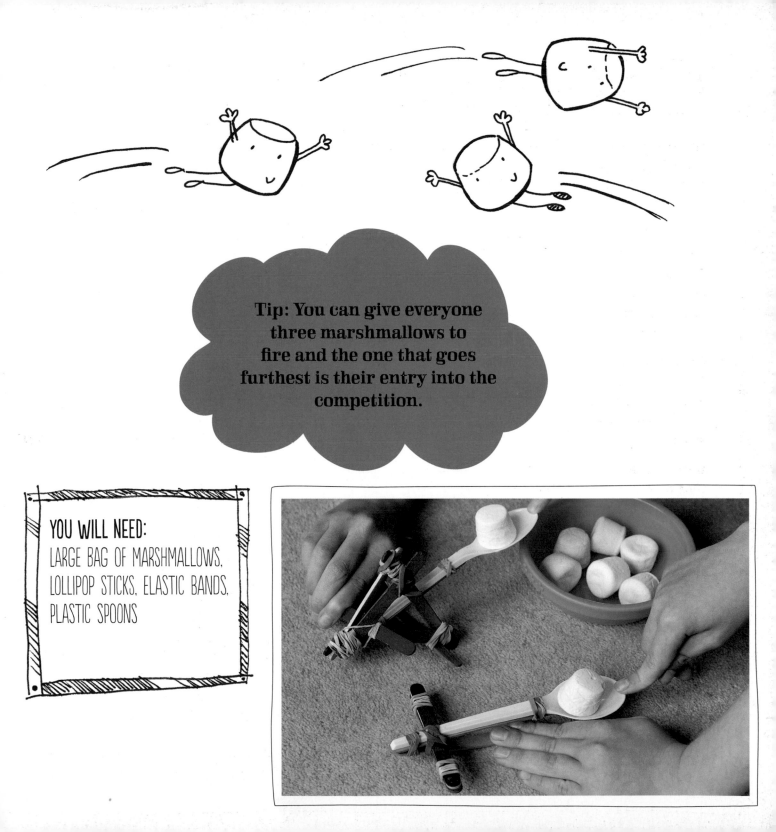

Tip: You can give everyone three marshmallows to fire and the one that goes furthest is their entry into the competition.

YOU WILL NEED:
LARGE BAG OF MARSHMALLOWS, LOLLIPOP STICKS, ELASTIC BANDS, PLASTIC SPOONS

Make wind instruments

I know you often make noise with your wind, but these sorts of wind instruments are a lot less smelly, easier to play and won't get you in so much trouble.

Straw panpipes

First, measure and cut your straws by lining them up next to a ruler, folding them at the correct point and then cutting along the crease. The first straw should be 19.5cm long, then the rest gradually get shorter with the measurements 17cm, 15.5cm, 14.5cm, 13cm, 11.5cm, 10cm and finally 9.5cm.

Keep hold of the offcut straws and use these as 'spacers' laid between the 'note' straws and set down about 3cm from the top. Use masking tape to join all the straws together, with the note straws running from longest to shortest and the spacers between them, then turn this structure over and wrap tape around the other side too.

The spacers mean you can blow across the top of a single straw – or note – at a time. Also, if you block the bottom of a straw as you blow, the note will be lowered, which will allow you to have two notes per straw and 16 altogether.

If you label your straws 1–8 (1 being the longest straw) you can have a go at playing these tunes (or composing your own).

Jingle Bells 333 / 333 / 35123 / 444 / 4433 / 3355421

Mary Had a Little Lamb 3212333 / 222 / 355 / 3212333 / 322321

Lollipop stick kazoo

Draw around one of your lollipop sticks on a piece of paper, cut out the shape and sandwich it between the two sticks. Use an elastic band to secure one end and then slip a piece of cocktail stick, just wider than the kazoo, underneath the paper next to the rubber band.

Add another cocktail stick at the other end, just above the paper this time, and again secure the end with an elastic band.

You can now make a buzzing sound by placing the kazoo between your lips and blowing or sucking. If you also press down on the sticks at the same time, you can make this sound go higher.

YOU WILL NEED FOR THE STRAW PANPIPES:
8 STRAWS, RULER, SCISSORS, MASKING TAPE

YOU WILL NEED FOR THE LOLLIPOP STICK KAZOO:
2 LOLLIPOP STICKS, PIECE OF PAPER, PENCIL, SCISSORS,
2 ELASTIC BANDS, 2 COCKTAIL STICKS

**Tip: Wider drinking straws
are easier to handle.**

Design your own board game

If you've had enough of sliding down snakes or going to jail without passing 'Go', it might be time to invent your own board game.

Start with a box. There will be lots of pieces to your game so it helps to have somewhere to store them. A good-sized shoebox works well – and don't forget, you can decorate it afterwards with the game's name.

To make the board, cut four thick pieces of white card. Each piece needs to be just smaller than the box itself. Lay them all out, face-down, so they make a larger square or rectangle and then use duct tape (or strong masking tape) to connect three of the four pieces. Double-check that this shape can now be folded away and will fit in the box.

On the front of the card, sketch out your game track in pencil from start to finish before dividing it into equal-sized 'spaces' for the players' tokens to jump along. The more spaces you have, the longer and more complex the game can be.

Now, liven things up by adding some hazards and bonuses. You could write these on specific spaces – for example, 'Go back 4 spaces' – or make a bunch of cards which players pick up when they land on a certain symbol. You can have separate symbols and piles for good and bad cards or mix them all up so it becomes a game of chance.

And, as it's your game, you can decide exactly what the cards say. Some might simply send you forwards or backwards a number of spaces, or you could add forfeits that players have to perform or questions they need to answer to move on.

You're now ready to decorate the board. If you want to personalise it, why not base the game around your favourite film, hobby, sport or perhaps places you like to visit? And remember, the cards can become part of the theme too and you can even make players' tokens to match, perhaps out of salt dough (see pages 96–97).

YOU WILL NEED: A BOX, THICK WHITE CARD, SCISSORS, DUCT TAPE (OR STRONG MASKING TAPE), PENCILS, FELT-TIP PENS OR PAINT (TO DECORATE), DICE, THIN CARD (FOR GAME CARDS), TOKENS OR COUNTERS

Make the board

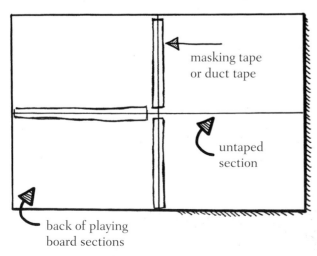

masking tape or duct tape

untaped section

back of playing board sections

Tip: Use a single dice so players can't move too many spaces in one go.

Tip: Test out your game a couple of times before finalising it to make sure you have the right balance of hazard and bonus spaces to keep things interesting.

Make an organiser

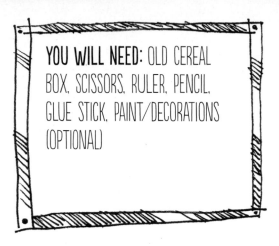

Yes, your room is an absolute tip but you and I both know it's not really your fault – you just need an organiser or two. To make one all you need is a cereal packet. NOOOO!! Wait! I meant an *empty* cereal packet.

Okay, so, once you've cleared up that cereal mess, you can get to work.

First, cut off the top flaps and lay the box down flat. Measure up 10cm on the left-hand side and make a mark with a pencil. Now, use your ruler to draw a diagonal line from this mark to the top right-hand corner.

Turn the box over and do the same on the other side, but this time measure 10cm from the bottom right-hand corner and join this up to the top left-hand corner. Finally, turn the box on its side and draw a straight line linking up the 10cm marks on both sides.

Take your scissors and cut along all the lines and you'll be left with the basic shape of your organiser. To make this structure stronger, take the section of the box you have cut away, turn it round and slot it into the organiser so it reinforces the bottom section of the structure. To secure it, run a glue stick along the top inside edge of this 'reinforcement' and press it against the inside wall of the organiser.

You can decorate your organiser by painting it (it may take several coats to cover over the cereal box pictures and writing) or adding paper patchwork or decoupage (pages 72–73).

And now, armed with your finished creation, you can rest safe in the knowledge that your room will never be messy again.*

* This might not actually be true. Sorry about that.

Tip: You can add labels to the front of your organisers so you know what you are keeping in each one.

Reinforcing your organiser

10cm

Hold a butter-making race

It is incredibly easy to make your own butter – all you need is some cream, a jar or container with a lid and a lot of shaking. To keep you going it's a good idea to make this a race – after all, there is nothing so motivating as the idea of beating your brother or sister.

Fill your container about a third full with the cream and put on the lid very securely. For the sake of fairness you should make sure you have containers of the same size and an equal amount of cream.

On 'Go' you can start shaking your containers. Just remember, this should be viewed as a marathon, not a sprint. Think about the hare and the tortoise (although don't forget to shake while you think or that pesky tortoise will steal the race again).

Within about 5 minutes, your cream will have become whipped and thick – but keep going. In about 10 minutes, you will suddenly start to hear liquid swishing around too – this is the buttermilk which has separated from the... BUTTER! Yes, that's right. It's over! You've won!

Now, do a victory lap around the kitchen before adding a pinch of salt to your butter, mixing it in and spreading this on a piece of victory toast.

YOU WILL NEED: 100ML WHIPPING CREAM (QUICKEST) OR DOUBLE CREAM (ADD ANOTHER 5 MINUTES OF SHAKING), CLEAN EMPTY JARS OR PLASTIC CONTAINERS WITH LIDS, PINCH OF SALT, VICTORY TOAST (OPTIONAL)

Tip: To save your arms you could make this a tag team race where partners take it in turns to shake for a minute each.

Tip: Your leftover buttermilk is perfect to use when making scones or muffins... which you can then spread with your homemade butter. Result!

Hold an indoor treasure hunt

YOU WILL NEED:
TREASURE, PAPER, PENCIL OR PEN, OLD TEA BAGS (OPTIONAL)

Before you begin organising this hunt, you'd better make sure you have some treasure to find. An ancient chest overflowing with gold and precious jewels might be a bit much to ask, but why not see if a grown-up can provide you with a few chocolates or sweets? If they seem reluctant, just remind them that this will keep you all occupied

for a good half an hour and it might suddenly seem worth providing a few small treats.

Now you need to think of some good hiding places. Try to come up with at least ten and use as many rooms as you can so your hunters are sent all over the house on their quest.

You will need to think of a clue to each location. The older the players, the harder the clues should be. For very young treasure hunters you can always use picture clues instead of written ones.

To give your clues an added sense of ancient mystery, tear around the edge of the paper, crumple it up, reopen it and rub an old, damp tea bag over it to give it an aged appearance.

Finally, you need to lay out your treasure trail. The easiest way to do this is working backwards, so begin by placing the treasure in the final spot. Take the clue for this location and hide it in another of your chosen spots. Keep doing this for all the clues until you are left with only one – this will be the starting clue you give to your players.

Oh, and don't forget to make it clear that you expect a cut of the treasure. A large cut.

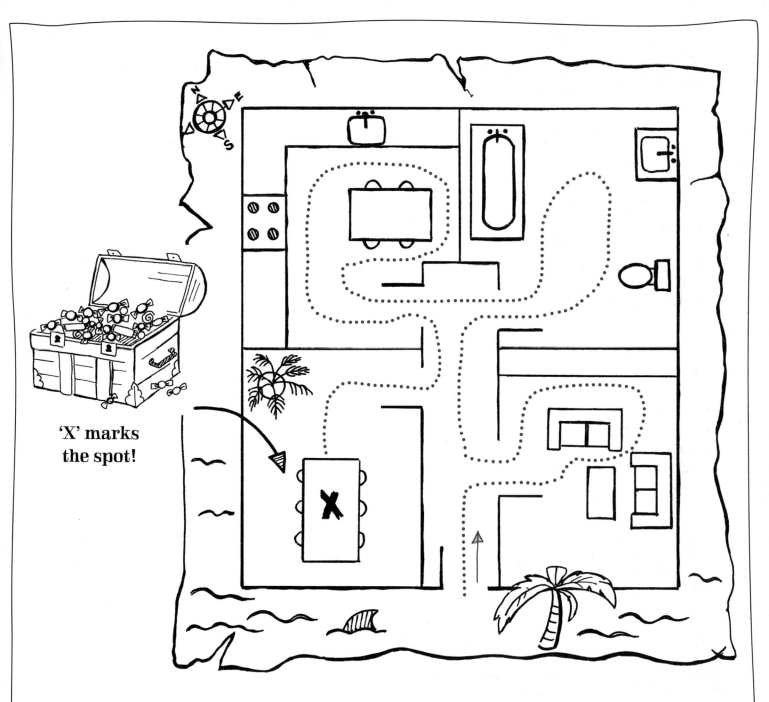

'X' marks the spot!

Tip: If you write different sets of clues, but each ending at the same final location, competing teams could race to find the treasure first.

Make a corner bookmark

1.

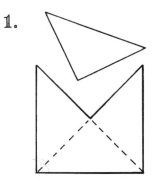

2.

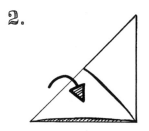

3.

Make corner bookmarks

So, let's say you're reading a fantastic book. Perhaps... oh, I don't know... *101 Things For Kids To Do On A Rainy Day* and you don't want to lose your place, or you need to mark something interesting. What do you do? NO! You do NOT fold down the corner of the page. Really! I despair of you sometimes.

Actually, the right answer is to use a bookmark. Thankfully, these are very easy to make and look fantastic so you've really no excuse for that page folding nonsense any more.

First, cut a square of paper – aim for 10.5cm x 10.5cm, as this size allows you to make four bookmarks from one sheet of A4.

Fold the bottom right-hand corner over to meet with the top left-hand corner. Unfold and repeat with the bottom left and top right. You should be left with four triangles marked out in creases.

Use scissors to cut out the top triangle. Next, fold the left-hand triangle over the middle one, add glue to the top of this and fold the right-hand triangle over and hold it down firmly for the glue to stick.

Now you just need to decorate your bookmark. Add eyes, nose and some teeth if you want to

make an animal or monster that looks like they are chewing your book. Alternatively, you could use pretty paper and embellish it with someone's initial, ribbons, sequins – whatever takes your fancy. In fact, these are so quick and easy you could make loads of different versions – after all, there's a lot of good stuff to mark in this book.

Tip: Make sure your bookmark decorations don't stick out too much or you will make indents in your book pages and I'll despair again.

Wrap a yarn tin vase

Tin cans are very tough and useful but they're not exactly gorgeous to look at. Do you know what they need? A nice bit of wool. Now if you want to knit them a lovely jumper that's fine by me, but it's a lot easier (and less weird) to just do a little bit of yarn wrapping.

First, make sure your tin can is clean and dry with its labels removed. If there are any sharp edges, ask a grown-up to rub them down carefully with some sandpaper.

Paste some PVA glue on the bottom section of the can and begin wrapping around it with wool. You don't want to see bits of can peeking through, so carefully push your coils of wool close together as you go.

When you feel like changing colour, simply cut your wool and tie on the next colour to this end. As you move up the can, keep adding more PVA glue to the tin and winding your wool over the top. Don't worry if you can see glue on the wool as this will disappear as it dries.

When you've covered the entire surface, cut your last bit of wool and tuck the end under the previous coils of wool using a pencil tip or cocktail stick to poke it down and do the same to the end at the bottom of the can.

Cut any long straggly ends off your tied knots and again poke the remaining wool under neighbouring coils. You are now left with a wool-covered can that you can use as a vase or pencil holder.

Tip: Make sure your wool ends and knots are all on the same side of the can so you have a super neat 'front'.

Tip: You can use this technique on almost any old container to give it a woolly makeover.

Make fifteens

Ever have problems remembering recipes? Then this is the one for you.

Begin by putting 15 digestive biscuits or another type of sweet crumbly biscuit in a freezer bag and use a rolling pin to roll and crush them up finely before pouring into a bowl.

Now, use clean scissors to cut 15 glacé cherries in half and 15 marshmallows into quarters, and add these to the crumbs. Mix these ingredients with a wooden spoon before pouring in the condensed milk and stirring everything together. You need to form a moist dough so if it's still a little dry, add a little more condensed milk.

Turn the dough out onto a clean work surface and roll it into a sausage shape. If you find it difficult to roll the dough in one, divide it in half and roll two shorter sausage shapes instead. Now, cut a piece of foil about twice the length of the dough sausage and sprinkle it with desiccated coconut. Take your sausage and roll it over the coconut until it's covered, then wrap it up in the foil and place it in the fridge to harden. I'm sorry but this bit will take a couple of hours – not 15 minutes.

When the sausage has hardened, take it out, unwrap it and slice it into 15 pieces (of course!).

Note: If you can't find condensed milk, beat together 2 eggs, 80g soft brown sugar, 1 tablespoon flour and ½ teaspoon vanilla extract and use this instead.

YOU WILL NEED: 15 DIGESTIVE BISCUITS, FREEZER BAG, ROLLING PIN, BOWL, SCISSORS, 15 GLACÉ CHERRIES, 15 LARGE MARSHMALLOWS, WOODEN SPOON, 150ML CONDENSED MILK (OR SEE NOTE ABOVE), KITCHEN FOIL, DESICCATED COCONUT, ROUND-ENDED KNIFE

Tip: If you want to make a melon basket, ask a grown-up to remove two wedges of melon from either side of the top to leave a 'handle' in place. You can use the extra melon flesh from these wedges to help make rainbow fruit kebabs (see pages 168–169).

Prepare a fruity melon bowl

There are many reasons to love melon bowls. You can use them for a glamorous breakfast dish, an impressive starter or a healthy pudding. They say 'Oh-my-goodness-you're-so-creative-in-the-kitchen', but actually are so easy you can knock one up in a few minutes – just don't tell anyone that. Best of all though, they are a dish which provides its own crockery – and that means less washing up. Result!

Start by asking a grown-up to slice a ripe melon in half and then get them to leave you in peace before they claim all the glory of this dish for themselves.

Next, scoop out the seeds and throw them away (or save a few for your scrap garden, see pages 118–119) before using a melon baller or teaspoon to take out rounded sections of melon flesh. Place these melon balls in a bowl as you go and keep scooping until you have a nice empty melon half.

You can now start refilling the melon by adding a few balls at a time alongside your chosen fruit – blueberries, raspberries, halved grapes and sliced strawberries all work well. Keep adding these until you've filled your melon case.

Now, take half an orange and squeeze the juice out of it, either using a juicer or your hands. Make sure there are no pips in this before pouring the juice over the fruit. Finally, serve with a sprig or two of mint and a smug smile at your own brilliance in the kitchen.

Tip: You can also check if someone is going into your drawers or cupboards by sticky taping a hair over the opening. If it's unstuck next time you check, you'll know an intruder has sneaked in.

Booby trap your bedroom

Younger brothers and sisters all seem to suffer from the same problems with their ears. Apparently, although you very clearly say 'DON'T go into my bedroom!' every day, what they hear is 'Please feel free to wander into my room at any time, and while you're there have a good look around and borrow anything you want.'

Well, here's a way to make them think twice.

Take a piece of masking tape or sticky tape and push a drawing pin through the middle from the sticky side to the outside. You can now fasten this to your door about 15–20cm from the hinge so the sharp end of the drawing pin is pointing out.

Next, blow up a balloon and fasten it with more masking tape to your bedroom wall, just behind your door, so the fattest part of the balloon is at the same level as the drawing pin.

Finally, open your door just enough to sneak out without letting the drawing pin touch the balloon.

Next time anyone enters your room the door will open onto the balloon so the drawing pin bursts it. This will be nice and loud, alerting you to the intruder – and testing their hearing at the same time.

YOU WILL NEED: MASKING TAPE (OR STICKY TAPE), DRAWING PIN, BALLOON

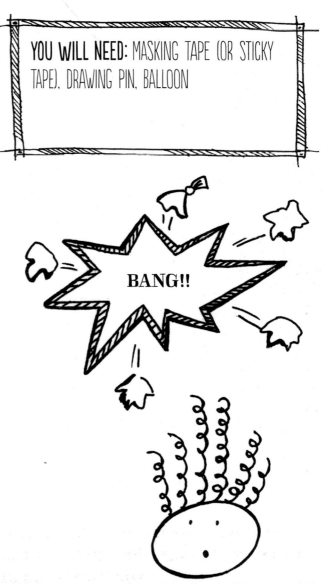

BANG!!

Play flap the fish

YOU WILL NEED:
NEWSPAPERS, PEN OR PENCIL, SCISSORS, MASKING TAPE OR STRING, COLOURED PAPER (OPTIONAL)

It's okay – no fish will be harmed in the playing of this game. This is because they are made out of paper, which is kinder – and a lot less smelly – than using real fish.

First, take the same number of newspaper sheets as you have players of the game and stack them on top of each other. Draw a simple fish shape on the top sheet and cut around it while holding all the sheets together to create a bunch of identical fish.

Each player takes a fish and a newspaper and must stand in a line at one end of the room. At the other end of the room is a finishing line marked out with masking tape or string.

On the word 'Go' everyone starts flapping behind their fish with the newspaper. The wafts of air will start to move the fish along and the first to cross the finishing line is declared the winner.

Players can also flap their opponents' fishes in the wrong direction if they are feeling particularly mischievous.

If you have a very small room you can race to the end of the room and back again to keep things going a little longer.

Tip: It can be helpful to write each player's name on their fish in case of multiple fish pile-ups, or use coloured paper instead of newspaper so each player has their own colour.

Create a word search

'What are you doing?'

'Oh, I'm just devising a word search.'

That's the really great thing about creating puzzles – they make you appear incredibly smart, but you leave the hard work of actually solving it to someone else. Which is... well... incredibly smart.

All you need for a word search is a piece of graph paper and a pen. If you can't get hold of any graph paper, just use a ruler and pencil to make a grid of your own (see crossword cards on pages 14–15).

Now, begin to write your words into the grid – remember, they can run up, down, from side to side or diagonally, and be written either forwards or backwards. Words can also cross over each other if they share a common letter.

As you add in your words, make sure you write them in a list at the bottom of the page so your 'searchers' know what to look for. You can theme the word search on anything you want – animals, friends' names, precious objects you have broken in the house in the last year, that kind of thing.

Finally, you need to 'hide' your words in a jumble of letters. Each empty grid space needs filling. It's a good idea to throw in some red herrings – for example, if one of your words is 'elephant' you can write one or two sections of the word elsewhere such as 'eleph'.

Your searcher can now look for all the hidden words, ringing each one as they find it. Feel free to stand behind them as they do this looking at your watch, rolling your eyes and occasionally tutting. That really helps pile on the pressure – although it might not do much for your friendship.

Tip: You and a friend could design a puzzle for each other and then see who can solve theirs first.

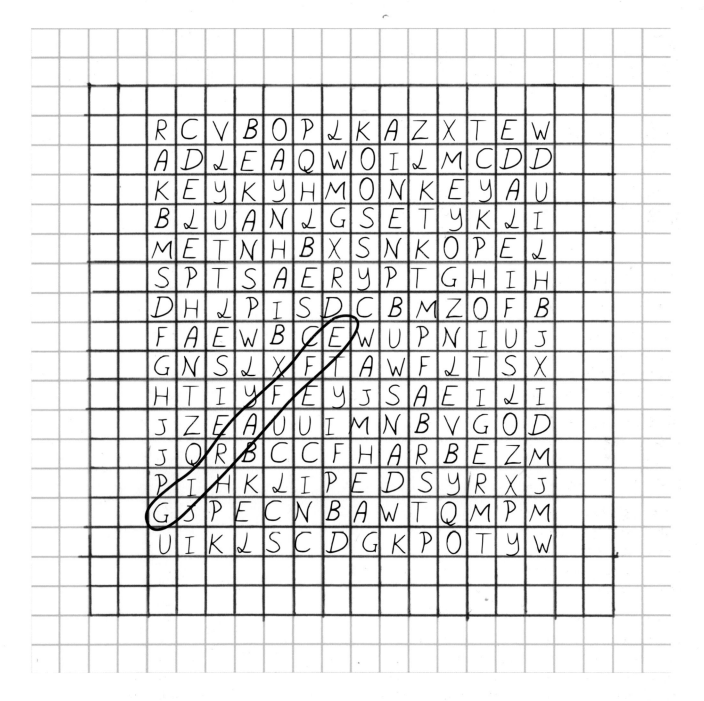

Words to find

Elephant, Snake, Giraffe, Monkey,
Lion, Tiger, Zebra

Construct a lava lamp

I had better warn you – this is not a lamp that you can read by or light your room with. In fact, it's no use as a lamp at all. But hey, it looks amazing, which is what really matters.

Make sure your bottle has all its labels removed (otherwise you won't even be able to see how amazing this looks and then it really is useless). Next, fill this three-quarters full with vegetable oil and add water until it almost reaches the top.

As water is denser than oil, it will make its way to the bottom of your lamp. You can now add several drops of food colouring to the bottle. This is water-based, so you can watch as it sinks through the oil to reach the water below, which it will then colour.

Now, carefully drop a quarter of an effervescent antacid tablet into the bottle.

As it hits the water it will begin to create carbon dioxide gas, which is even lighter than the oil so floats to the top – but, handily, this will attach itself to blobs of the coloured water, so you will see this rise too. When the coloured water hits the top it will sink back again.

When the bubbles stop you can add another piece of antacid tablet to start the reaction again. Also, you can put the lid on your bottle and tip it back and forth to make a coloured wave which also looks pretty... well... amazing.

YOU WILL NEED: 1 LITRE EMPTY BOTTLE, VEGETABLE OIL, WATER, FOOD COLOURING, EFFERVESCENT ANTACID TABLET (OR PIECE OF BATH BOMB)

Tip: You can keep your lava lamp for re-use – just pop the lid back on and make sure no one mistakes it for a weird new drink.

Tip: Small pieces of bath bombs (see pages 12–13) are a useful alternative to the antacid tablets.

Prepare fresh strawberry tiramisu

This recipe involves separating egg whites and yolks, so either you learn this skill quickly or you're going to be eating a lot of scrambled eggs and omelettes.

First, you'll need three bowls – one for breaking eggs, one for whites and one for yolks. Carefully, tap an egg on the edge of the breaking bowl so you're striking it right along its centre. If it cracks nicely, quickly turn the egg halves upwards so you have two little cups. If it only partly breaks, gently try to get your thumbs into this hole and split the egg open – again quickly holding the egg halves upwards.

If the yolk is still in one piece, you need to start tipping this carefully from one egg half to the other, holding it over the bowl. Bit by bit the egg white will drip into the bowl, leaving you with just the yolk. Transfer the egg yolk and whites to their separate bowls and repeat with the other egg.

Take the yolks bowl and sift in the icing sugar before slowly stirring the mixture all together with a wooden spoon until it's nice and fluffy. Then, stir in the mascarpone.

Now turn your attention to the egg whites bowl. Start whisking the egg whites until they change from a see-through liquid to fluffy white peaks (this takes about 10 minutes – or a lot less if you use an electric whisk). Pour in the mascarpone-and-yolk mixture and use a metal spoon to mix and fold this into the egg whites.

Pour the orange juice into another bowl (yes, we are making a lot of washing up here – but don't worry, it'll be so delicious the grown-ups won't care... much) and quickly dip in a few sponge fingers before laying them in the bottom of your serving dish. Next, add fresh strawberries (with the green stalk removed and the fruit cut in half) and then a layer of the mascarpone mixture. Keep repeating these layers until you've used up all the ingredients.

Finally, place it in the fridge to chill for 2–3 hours (which should give you just enough time to wash up all those bowls).

YOU WILL NEED: 4 BOWLS, 2 EGGS, 50G ICING SUGAR, SIEVE, WOODEN SPOON, 150G MASCARPONE, WHISK, METAL SPOON, 150ML ORANGE JUICE, MEASURING JUG, 9 SPONGE FINGERS (LADY FINGERS), 150G STRAWBERRIES, SERVING DISH (1 LITRE), EXTRA STRAWBERRIES AND CHOCOLATE SPRINKLES (TO DECORATE THE TOP)

Tip: You can top the final layer of mascarpone with some whole strawberries for an impressive garnish and even add some chocolate sprinkles.

Separating eggs can be a tricky business.

Make a fortune-teller

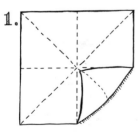
1.

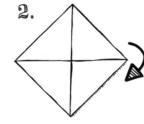
2.

3.

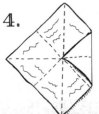
4.

5.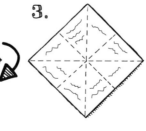

6.

YOU WILL NEED: SQUARE OF PAPER, COLOURED PENS, PENCILS OR CRAYONS, PEN OR PENCIL

Fold an origami fortune-teller

If you've accidentally misplaced your crystal ball, don't worry. You can create your own 100 per cent accurate* fortune-teller using paper and pens.

Take a square of paper, fold the base to the top, add a crease, open it and then do the same in the other direction. Next, create two diagonal lines by folding the bottom right-hand corner to the top left, creasing, unfolding and repeating with the bottom left-hand corner to the top right.

Bring the bottom right corner into the centre and press it flat before doing the same for the other three (diagrams 1–2).

Flip this square over and you'll see a crease pattern with eight separate triangles where you can write your fortunes (diagram 3):

Don't count on it

Yes

Most likely

Very unlikely

No

Ask again later

Decidedly no

The outlook is good

Now, fold the bottom right-hand corner in to the centre and press flat, before repeating this for the other three. Again you will see eight triangles – on these write the numbers 1–8 (diagrams 4–5).

Turn over the square and add a coloured circle – red, yellow, green, blue – to each of the four square flaps. Prise these open so you can fit in a thumb to each of the front two and your index fingers to the back pair (diagram 6).

Now your friends can ask their question and choose a colour – if it's blue you need to move the fortune-teller four times for 'B' 'L' 'U' 'E'. First, open it like a mouth but keep your fingers together and your thumbs together. Next time open it in the other direction by keeping your thumb and finger on each hand together – each 'open' counts as one move.

On the last count keep the fortune-teller open to reveal four numbers – your friend should choose one so you can move your fortune-teller that number of times. Finally, when it opens again, they choose another number, which you lift up to reveal the answer to their question beneath.

* I have completely made this up (which you would have been able to predict had you used your fortune-teller).

Build a marble run

If you think you're a fast mover, you should watch a marble go. In fact, you can do just that by building a homemade marble run. Then you could try to race them (but my money's still on the marble).

First, you'll need to decide where to build your marble run. By the side of stairs is ideal but equally you could use a section of empty wall or a tall cupboard or door and use a chair to help you reach the higher points in your run.

You'll need to gather together lots of building materials. Empty cardboard tubes of all sizes are great, but you can also cut the tops off plastic bottles and turn them upside down to make some chutes.

If you are using tubes it can help to cut out a tongue shape at the top so the marble has a space to drop into. You can also add wide slits and tunnel-shaped openings into their sides so you can feed in the ends of other tubes.

Attach your sections to your wall using masking tape (this won't mark the paint and is easy to take off and put on) and keep testing with marbles as you go to make sure the run works.

You can add a large collecting pot or box at the base of your run to catch all the marbles as you go.

Tip: Marbles left on stairs or the floor are not a good idea, so always make sure you pick up or collect each marble as it comes down the run.

A large funnel shape
or chute at the start
makes it easier to
drop in a marble.

Set up an indoor obstacle course

The next time a grown-up moans at you for leaving cushions scattered all over the floor or your toys in a mess, here is the perfect answer – no, of course you weren't being untidy, you were just inventing a new obstacle course.

And as well as being a super-handy excuse, indoor obstacle courses can also be a great way to spend a wet afternoon.

You can be as creative as you want when inventing your course. Chairs are great for climbing over or crawling through. Or you can place them slightly apart, backs facing each other, and throw a blanket or sheet over the top to make your own tunnel.

A blanket on the floor weighted down at the edges makes a homemade crawl net and you could place cushions some distance apart, then get people to leap between them.

If you have a narrow corridor, why not get some wool and masking tape and create your own spy web for players to negotiate. If you touch the 'lasers' it's back to the start.

To prevent collisions you can time players on how long it takes them to complete the course, with time penalties awarded for any failed tasks. The winner gets the glory, the losers get to clear up.

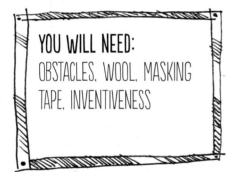

YOU WILL NEED:
OBSTACLES, WOOL, MASKING TAPE, INVENTIVENESS

Tip: To include some target practice in your obstacle course, place a pile of soft toys at a line of masking tape and try to lob them into buckets at a distance.

Launch a Magnus glider

This is called a Magnus glider because it uses the Magnus force (and that is something that causes spinning balls to bend and lift in the air and not a small army led by someone called Magnus... in case you were wondering).

First, you'll need sticky tape or masking tape to join together the bases of the two polystyrene cups. These sort of cups work best because their slightly textured surface helps the force work, they're extremely light, which means the force will have a greater effect – oh, and they don't hurt when they hit someone on the head by accident (which gets you in a lot less trouble).

Now, make your launcher. Place one elastic band on the table, then place a second so it overlaps the first one halfway along. Lift up the first band where it overlaps so you can reach for the second one underneath and then pull the second band through on itself so it forms a knot between the two. Keep doing this until you have a length of elastic band chain about 30–40 cm long.

Using your thumb hold the end of your elastic band chain in the middle of the glider where the two cups join. Now, wrap it round itself once or twice so the end is held in place. Stretch the elastic as you do this to give you more force.

Finally, hold the end of the band away from you and stretched out while holding the cups against you. Make sure that the elastic band chain is coming out from underneath the glider, not above it. Now, let go, aiming the glider slightly upwards and watch it spin and float through the air as the Magnus force creates an uplift. It can take some practice to get the technique perfected but when you do, you should find your glider will fly for several seconds at a time.

Tip: You can decorate your glider with markers, acrylic paint pens or stickers.

Make the glider and launcher

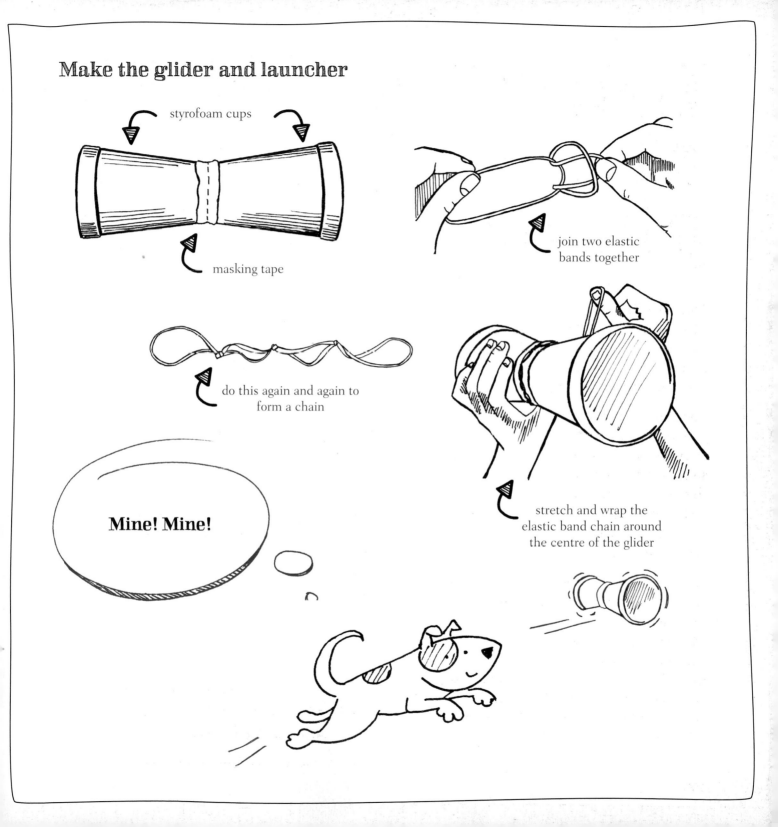

styrofoam cups

masking tape

join two elastic bands together

do this again and again to form a chain

stretch and wrap the elastic band chain around the centre of the glider

Mine! Mine!

Build a solar system mobile

When it comes to craft projects, it's good to think big – and it doesn't get much bigger than the solar system. Thankfully, this is a scaled-down model, so there's no need to extend your bedroom just yet.

Start with a large square of card, at least 45cm across. Locate its centre using a ruler and push through a sharp pencil into an eraser beneath to make a hole.

Keep the pencil there and tie on a piece of string. Measure this out so it reaches the edge of the cardboard and tie this end to the other pencil. Move the second pencil around while holding the middle one still and they'll act as a compass allowing you to create a circle.

Draw seven more, with the circle getting smaller each time, to mark the orbits of the planets. Cut around the largest circle before making a hole somewhere along each line of orbit. Finally, paint it all black, and when dry add white dots for stars.

Make the sun and planets using coloured card: yellow (sun), orange (Venus), white, orange and brown (Jupiter), yellow and brown (Saturn), grey (Mercury), red (Mars), blue-green (Uranus), blue (Neptune) and blue and green (Earth). Make the sun the largest, Saturn and Jupiter the next biggest, Neptune and Uranus a little smaller,

Solar system mobile

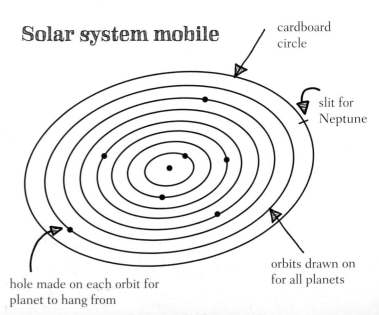

cardboard circle

slit for Neptune

orbits drawn on for all planets

hole made on each orbit for planet to hang from

Earth and Venus a size below these and Mercury and Mars smaller still.

For each planet, place three card circles on top of each other, staple down the centre line, then punch a hole near the top before folding out the circles to create the 3D shape.

Thread a piece of wool through the hole, tie a knot, and thread the other end through the correct orbit hole above. For Neptune, cut a slit on the edge of the space disc to pass the wool through. Tie the ends together above the central disc so they can't escape.

Now, make three holes evenly spaced around the edge of the space disc, tie each with a length of wool and bring the three ends together. Make sure when you hold all three that the space disc is level before tying them together in a knot and then attaching a short length of string or ribbon to form an 'eye'. Ask a grown-up to hang this eye from a ceiling fixing so you can admire your brilliant handiwork.

From the sun, the order of the planets is Mercury, Venus, Earth, Mars, Jupiter, Saturn, Uranus and Neptune.

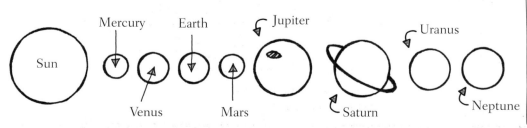

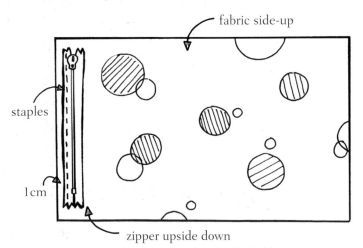

Tip: Don't get the staples or duct tape too near the zip teeth or they will catch in them when you try to move the zip.

Making your pencil case

fabric side-up

staples

1cm

zipper upside down

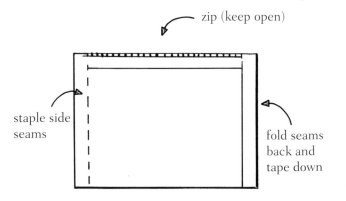

zip (keep open)

staple side seams

fold seams back and tape down

Make a no-sew pencil case

If you haven't got a sewing machine (or if you do but your parents have told you quite pointedly that you are NOT having a go on it), this is the ideal project for you – a no-sew pencil case.

First, you'll need a zip. You can buy these but it's cheaper if you can recycle one from old clothing that's on its way out. Ideally, it should be at least 20cm long as this will fit most pens and pencils.

Now, prepare your fabric. You will need a rectangular piece 3cm wider than the zip and about 30cm long. Cut it out and coat the back in duct tape, overlapping each piece slightly and trimming off any excess at the end (see pages 92–93).

Using a ruler and ballpoint pen, draw a line 1.5cm in from the edge of the duct tape side, all the way around – this is your 'seam allowance' (you see, even without a sewing machine you can use all sorts of fancy terms).

Place your zip upside down on the outer fabric so it sits 1cm down from the top of your rectangle. Then, flip it over and staple the zip to the fabric using the pen line as a guide.

Fold the fabric in half (duct tape facing outwards), open the zip and line up the unstapled side of the zip 1cm down from the opposite edge of the fabric and staple this as you did the other.

Next, staple both sides shut by following the seam lines. Use duct tape to tape over any raw edges as well as the staples near the zip.

Finally, turn the bag the right way out and it's ready to use – or just show it to your parents and watch their faces turn pale as they wonder how on earth you found the sewing machine they thought they'd hidden. Mwa, ha, ha.

YOU WILL NEED: ZIP, FABRIC, SCISSORS, DUCT TAPE, PEN, RULER, STAPLER

Create pinwheel sandwiches

I have no idea why sandwiches taste better in a swirl, but they do. It's a fact.

If you want to test out this theory yourself (although really you should just believe me – I'm always right), you'll need some really fresh, thinly sliced, soft bread. Cut off the crusts carefully (get an adult to do this if your knife skills are at all dodgy) and add a thin layer of soft butter or margarine.

You can use any fillings you want but remember the sandwiches need to roll, so it's best to use something that spreads or is very small or thin.

If you're doing these for a lot of people, you could use lots of different fillings for variety.

You could make savoury sandwiches, such as tuna mayonnaise and sweetcorn, thinly sliced ham, soft cheese and cucumber slices. Or sweet ones using things like jam, peanut butter or honey. Or you can get as creative as you like (although I would avoid tuna with Marmite and peanut butter – it is as bad as it sounds). Also, it's best to avoid wet fillings, such as tomatoes, or you'll get soggy pinwheels – and no amount of swirl will make that look appetising.

When you've added your filling, simply roll up your sandwich, starting at one end and keeping the roll as tight as possible. When you're done, wrap it tightly in clingfilm and put it in the fridge to chill for at least an hour.

Finally, take it out and slice each roll into five pinwheels which you should display, whirl-up, on plates.

YOU WILL NEED: SOFT SLICED BREAD, KNIFE (GROWN-UP TO SUPERVISE), BUTTER OR MARGARINE, FILLINGS, CLINGFILM, PLATE

Tip: You can add two or three different pinwheels to a skewer on a bed of lettuce for a really fancy display.

Play shadow charades

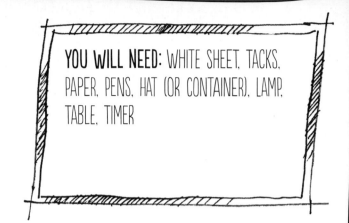

YOU WILL NEED: WHITE SHEET, TACKS, PAPER, PENS, HAT (OR CONTAINER), LAMP, TABLE, TIMER

This is very like normal charades but a bit more difficult. Hang on – that doesn't sound good, does it? Okay – it's very like normal charades but you can pull faces at people and they'll never know. That's better.

Begin by hanging a white sheet over a doorway. Unless you've had a growth spurt, you'll need a grown-up to help with this. They can attach it with masking tape but it's best to use small tacks pressed into the top of the doorframe.

If they're worried by this idea, remind them that no one looks at the top of doorframes and anyway, the thick layer of dust up there should cover the holes afterwards (they might not like you insulting their housekeeping skills but they'll find it hard to argue with the logic).

Split into two teams and ask someone who isn't playing to write words for you to act out. These could be things like actions (applause, sneeze, dig); objects (escalator, robot, banana) or even animals and people (monkey, elephant, cat, Great Uncle Tobias). The clues are folded and put into a hat (or something similar).

Now, put a lamp with the lampshade removed on a table a couple of metres behind the sheet and turn off all the other lights (and shut the curtains if it's not quite dark).

A player in the first team now picks out a clue from the hat, gets behind the sheet and on 'Go' begins to act out the word. Remember, the clue giver can't make a sound and no one will be able to see anything but the shadow they create.

The first team has a minute to guess the answer. If they don't get it, the second team has one guess and if they're right they 'steal' the point.

Next, the second team puts forward a player and the game continues until everyone has had a go, or as many rounds as you decide to play, or until someone catches you pulling faces at them from behind the sheet and leaves the room in a huff.

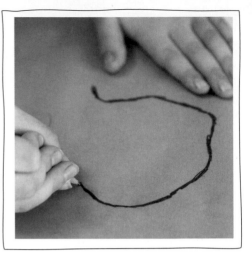

Tip: Secure your tracing paper with tape to stop it moving while you draw in the line and also when you transfer it to the black card.

Create silhouette portraits

'You've made my eyes look weird.'

'Why is my nose wonky?'

'My hair is NOTHING like that.'

This is the problem when you're drawing someone's picture – they get all fussy about it needing to look like them.

You can solve a lot of these problems by making a silhouette portrait. Not only will it be very classy and professional, there's also no need to bother putting in lots of details.

The key is having a great photograph of your subject with their head in profile (sideways on). The bigger this photograph is, the better, as it will be easier to work with. And if you don't have a photo you can always look for a profile picture of someone in a magazine or newspaper.

Now, place your tracing paper over the picture and very carefully use a pencil to mark a line around the outside of the face and back of the head. Make sure you get the neck or shoulders in too.

Turn this tracing paper over onto some black card and, using the pencil again, scribble over the back of all the lines you traced. This will transfer the original pencil marks onto the black card, which

you will see when you lift off the tracing paper. When it comes to the neck and shoulders, add another pencil line that makes a gentle curve from the back to the front. Then take your scissors and cut along all the lines.

Next, cut a circle from a white or brightly coloured piece of card, a little larger than the portrait. Cut another circle, larger again, from some black card and stick the first circle onto the centre of this. Finally, turn over the black silhouette, so it is again facing the right way and stick it in the middle of the white or coloured paper. You will now have a perfect silhouette portrait in a beautiful frame and, for once, no one can tell you that their eye colour is wrong, their hair is a mess or their nostrils look as big as caves.

YOU WILL NEED: PHOTOGRAPH OR PICTURE IN PROFILE, TRACING PAPER, PENCIL, BLACK CARD, SCISSORS, WHITE OR BRIGHTLY COLOURED CARD, GLUE STICK

Make rainbow fruit kebabs

Fruit really knows how to draw attention to itself. It's always hanging about looking brightly coloured and delicious... the show off! Still, it does make it perfect for creating eye-catching food – like rainbow fruit kebabs.

First, find a big plate and slice up your melon (you should get a grown-up to help with this as rolling fruit and sharp knives are not a great combination). Cut it in half lengthways and then each piece in half lengthways again to give you four segments – or hills.

Place one 'hill' at the back, two in front of this and one centrally in front of these to create a rolling hills landscape.

You can use different fruits for rainbow colours depending on what's around:

Red – strawberries, raspberries, watermelon

Orange – Cantaloupe melon, tangerines, satsumas or... ummm... oranges

Yellow – pineapple, mangoes

Green – honeydew melon, kiwi, green grapes

Blue/indigo – blueberries (yes, that colour's a bit limited)

Violet – red grapes (and that one's not giving us a lot of options either)

Some fruit needs preparing, such as taking the green stalks off strawberries or peeling and cutting kiwis. If you want to cut down on your work, use whole berries and tangerines or satsuma slices that you can prepare without needing to cut.

When your fruit is ready just thread pieces onto the kebab skewers in the order of the rainbow and leave plenty of space on the skewer below your last purple fruit.

Now, place your skewers in the back 'hill'. It's easiest to start with the middle skewer straight up and then add skewers down the sides, each one at a slightly larger angle to create a rainbow effect.

And finally, don't forget to add a pot of gold. To do this, fill a small dish or bowl with some yogurt or crème fraîche and place it at one end of your rainbow before presenting your finished work of food art to the family. You could even yell 'Look at me! Look at what I've made!'

After all, fruit shouldn't be the only one allowed to show off.

Tip: Anything that needs cutting up should be a similar size to other fruit you might be using, such as grapes or strawberries.

Tip: If you don't have a cantaloupe melon you could use another type of melon or even a watermelon (this is very big so you will probably only need one single hill).

YOU WILL NEED: LARGE PLATE, CANTALOUPE MELON, SHARP KNIFE (FOR GROWN-UP TO USE), COLOURFUL FRUIT, WOODEN KEBAB SKEWERS, SMALL POT OR DISH, YOGURT OR CRÈME FRAÎCHE

Play the glasses

Grown-ups are funny sometimes. First, they say how important it is for kids to learn a musical instrument, but the moment you pick up a recorder or drum they run out of the room.

Luckily, the glasses are slightly quieter than drums and a little easier to play than the recorder.

To begin with, you'll need to find some glasses. If they're ones you use every day that's probably okay, but avoid precious wedding gifts, family heirlooms or anything with a stem – and always check with a grown-up first.

Glasses of the same size and shape are easiest to use but don't be put off if you have a random mixture – it will just take a little longer to tune them.

If you have a set of the same glasses, leave one empty as the base note and then get a jug with water and start filling the others. Each one should have a little more water in than the one before. Now, take a pencil and gently strike the glasses on their side in order. As you hit them, those with more water will make a higher note.

If you have an odd assortment of glasses strike each one when empty and work out which order they go in, from lowest note to highest. If there is only a small difference between two of the glasses, add water to one to get a more even run of notes.

When you feel you have a good glass xylophone you can start to work out some simple tunes – Twinkle Twinkle Little Star or Happy Birthday work well. Also, you can use food colouring to dye each glass of water a different colour and then start writing up tunes in colour codes. Before you know it, you'll be composing glass xylophone symphonies and jamming with the biggest bands in the world. Maybe.

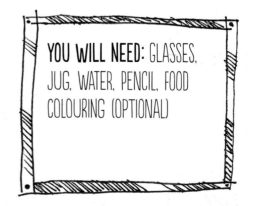

YOU WILL NEED: GLASSES, JUG, WATER, PENCIL, FOOD COLOURING (OPTIONAL)

Craft with papier mâché

Papier mâché comes from the French phrase meaning 'chewed paper'.

STOP! Spit it out! I was giving you a bit of background – not an instruction. Let's start again.

The first thing you'll need for creating papier mâché is some torn newspaper (not chewed). Rip strips about 2–3 cm wide and 10cm long, but don't worry if they are a little bigger or smaller.

Make your paste by mixing a cup of flour and a cup and a half of water together or by diluting two parts PVA glue with one part water. Make sure it's mixed to a nice smooth consistency.

Now, decide what you want to make. A blown-up balloon can be a useful base for many structures. Just paint your strips either side with paste or dip in your newspaper and then remove the excess paste by pulling it through your fingers and sticking it to the balloon.

When you've built up enough layers and it's dry, you can pop the balloon by poking through a pin or needle and you'll be left with the structure. If you want to use this to make a piñata that can be broken afterwards, four layers is enough, but for stronger structures you need at least double this. Just remember, when you've put on three layers to a structure, let your papier mâché dry before you add more.

To make a bowl or plate, use a real one as a mould, coat it in foil so it can be removed afterwards and papier mâché on top of it or, if it's a flexible plastic bowl, you can papier-mâché directly onto it. If you want to add a handle to a bowl, use masking tape to attach a cardboard version that you can then overcoat with papier mâché.

Cardboard shapes attached with masking tape are a good way to build up more complex structures and with papier mâché, it's possible to make all sorts of items – animal models, jewellery, masks, money boxes, castles... anything really (but not snacks – so please stop chewing that paper!).

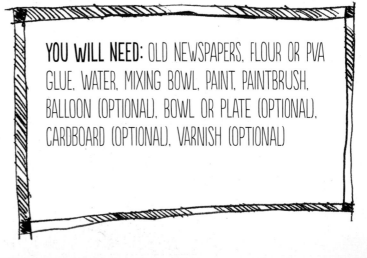

YOU WILL NEED: OLD NEWSPAPERS, FLOUR OR PVA GLUE, WATER, MIXING BOWL, PAINT, PAINTBRUSH, BALLOON (OPTIONAL), BOWL OR PLATE (OPTIONAL), CARDBOARD (OPTIONAL), VARNISH (OPTIONAL)

Tip: Use varnish to give your piece a nice shine and make it more waterproof – or just a layer of PVA glue.

Run your own library

Not only will this stop people borrowing your books and forgetting to give them back, it will also allow you to say 'Shush' very loudly and impose large fines on anyone who dares to return a book late.* Who knew running a library could be this much fun?

First, you should probably add a bit of order to your bookshelves. To make it easier for people to browse you could divide them into 'fiction' and 'non-fiction' sections and then arrange the books alphabetically by authors' surnames. Then again, you could simply organise them by colour of book spine or size of book – after all, it's your library.

If you add stickers to the insides of your books declaring them 'Property of' your library that'll help make sure they're returned. And to create a pouch to keep borrowing records in, just draw a template like the one opposite on a piece of thin card, cut it out, then fold and glue the tabs. You can stick one of these in the front page of each book with glue or double-sided sticky tape.

Now, cut slips of lined paper measuring 10cm x 7cm. Write the book title and author at the top then draw in two columns. Head a wider column 'Borrower' and a narrower column 'Date Due'. This way each time that book is borrowed, you can write in who has taken it and when you expect it back. Oh, and as you can never trust brothers or sisters to check this, you should also make a note in your own library record notebook.

And there's no need to stop there. You could set out a reading area for people who want to browse books before they borrow, 'Book of the Week' displays to recommend your favourite reads to others and 'Book Jail' for anyone who loses one of your books.

* Not that this means they will ever pay them... but imposing them is still fun.

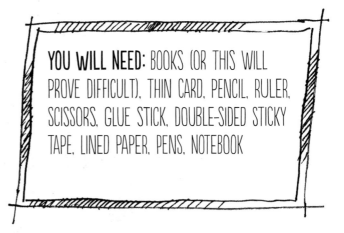

YOU WILL NEED: BOOKS (OR THIS WILL PROVE DIFFICULT), THIN CARD, PENCIL, RULER, SCISSORS, GLUE STICK, DOUBLE-SIDED STICKY TAPE, LINED PAPER, PENS, NOTEBOOK

Make a records pouch

8cm

12cm

fold up
lower section

8cm

1cm

fold in tabs
and glue in
place

Tip: You can design your own library cards to give to anyone you feel worthy of using your library.

Sshhh!

Erupt a volcano

With their pesky habit of throwing out rocks, molten lava and poisonous gases, it's tricky to watch volcanoes erupt. You can solve this problem by simply building your own and exploding it at will.

First, use masking tape to connect the base of your plastic bottle to the centre of a large piece of cardboard and then longer tape strips to join the top of the bottle to the edge of the cardboard in several places. Now, scrunch up newspaper and slip it under the tape to build up the shape of the mountain. Don't worry if the masking tape comes away – just restick it or add a bit more to roughly hold the newspaper in place.

When you're happy with the shape, take some ripped-up newspapers – about a quarter of a sheet in size – and coat the back of them with a papier mâché mixture (two parts PVA glue, one part water). Stick these over the top to create the mountain surface. You may need to add a couple of layers and then finish with smaller ripped strips that you can mould to give the surface a craggier look.

After a couple of hours, the structure should be dry enough to paint. Use dark browns and greys as a base colour and you can also add fiery details of reds, oranges and yellows for added drama.

Finally, add several drops of red food colouring to 300ml of warm water as well as 200ml of vinegar and a tablespoon of washing-up liquid. Give it a stir and then, using a funnel, pour this mixture into the top of your volcano (the mouth of your plastic bottle) and put on the lid.

When you're ready to erupt the volcano, place it on a wipeable tablecloth (flowing lava can be a bit messy) and place two tablespoons of bicarbonate of soda on a folded piece of card. Remove the lid of the bottle and use the chute formed from the folded card to quickly deliver all of your bicarbonate of soda inside the volcano.

Now, stand back as the lava bubbles up from inside your bottle and flows down the side of your mountain. And if you want to make it even more authentic, you could eat lots of beans and let off some noxious fumes of your own.

YOU WILL NEED: MASKING TAPE, 1 LITRE PLASTIC BOTTLE WITH LID, LARGE PIECE OF CARDBOARD, NEWSPAPER, MEASURING JUG, PVA GLUE, WATER, PAINT, PAINTBRUSH, RED FOOD COLOURING, WARM WATER, VINEGAR, WASHING UP LIQUID, FUNNEL, WIPEABLE TABLECLOTH, BICARBONATE OF SODA, CARD

Tip: If you coat your mountain in PVA glue and let it dry this will protect the surface and allow you to explode your volcano again another day after mopping up the lava and emptying the bottle by tipping the volcano over a sink.

If you don't have any newspaper, any thin scrunched up paper will do.

Learn a magic trick

YOU WILL NEED: RUBBER BAND (FOR 'MAKE A RUBBER BAND JUMP'); KETCHUP/SAUCE SACHET, PLASTIC BOTTLE WITH LID (FOR 'MIND CONTROL'); WATER, A4 OR A5 SHEET OF PAPER, SCISSORS (FOR 'STEP THROUGH A PIECE OF PAPER')

You'll know when you have mastered these tricks because people will say 'WOW, that's amazing!' immediately followed by 'How does it work?'.

WARNING: answering the second will mean they never say the first one again.

Make a rubber band jump

Place a small rubber band over your index and middle finger and clench your fist so it faces the audience. They will only be able to see the rubber band at the base of your fingers but on the other side make sure that all four finger tips are hooked into the band too. Now, open up your hand and the rubber band will jump over to your other two fingers. Incredible!

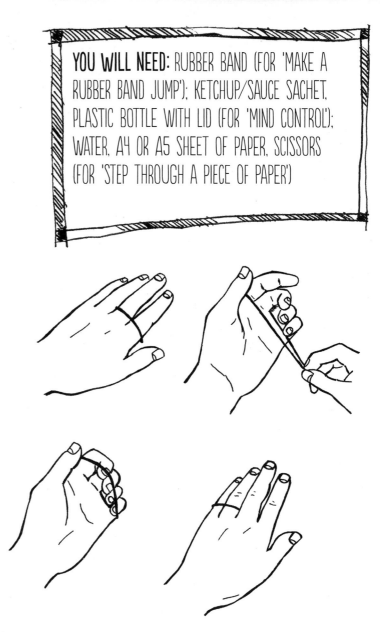

Tip: If you don't have a rubber band to hand, hair bobbles can also work for this trick.

Mind control

You'll need a small sachet of ketchup or sauce for this – the type you are given in cafés. Pop this in an empty plastic bottle and fill it almost to the top with water and put on the lid.

Now for the clever part: place one hand around the middle of the bottle while you move the other one up and down in the air, pretending to control the movement of the packet. This also helps distract your audience because as you move this hand, you will actually be controlling the packet with your other.

Yes, by gently squeezing the bottle you can make the packet rise and letting it go will mean it sinks. If you practise, you can even get it to stay part way up or down the bottle. Amazing!

Step through a piece of paper

Holding a piece of paper, announce to your audience that you can cut a hole in it large enough for you to walk through.

Fold the paper in half lengthways and cut from the folded line down to the edge about 1cm wide but stopping short of the end so the paper remains in one piece.

Quickly carry on adding these cuts every centimetre or so, first from the outside edge towards the inside and then the inside towards the outside. Make sure the last cut goes from the folded edge towards the outside of the paper.

Cut along the fold line but make sure you leave the first and last folded section intact. Finally, open out the shape to reveal a circle large enough for you to step though.

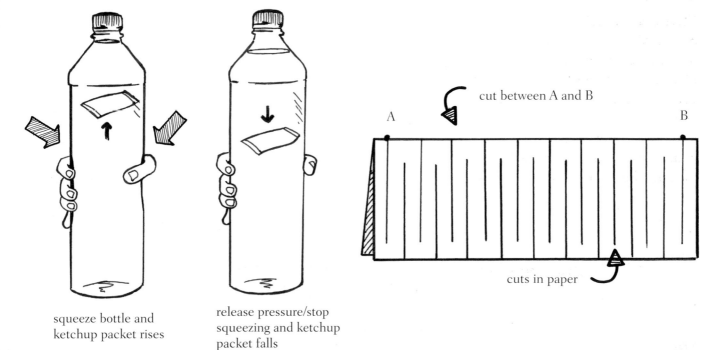

squeeze bottle and ketchup packet rises

release pressure/stop squeezing and ketchup packet falls

cut between A and B

A   B

cuts in paper

Decorate a tablecloth

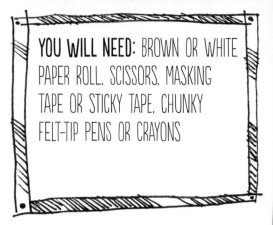
As this is a paper cloth you'll use it only once – unless you have perfect table manners and never spill or drop a thing when you eat. Exactly. As I said: you can use it once.

First, position your roll of paper on the table so it overhangs one end by about 20–30cm and then unroll it until it reaches the other. Here, put a small fold on one edge to mark the paper, then move it back onto the table, make a nice long fold at the mark and cut there.

Unless you have very wide paper – or a narrow table – you'll need to join together more than one piece to make the cloth. To do this find a clear piece of floor and roll out your cut paper, weighting it down at both ends with something heavy to stop it rolling back up. Take the rest of the roll, line it up with the cut paper at one end, weight it down and unroll it so it's in line with the other end. Now, carefully fold and cut this end of the roll.

Position your two lengths, upper side to the floor, so they just overlap along the middle line by a couple of centimetres. Place some more weights on the paper to keep it nice and flat and stick these pieces together with a line of tape. Finally, roll the whole thing up and take it back to lay on the table where you can keep it in place with a little more tape to stop it moving while you decorate.

Use chunky felt-tip pens or wax crayons to embellish your cloth. You could make place settings by drawing around plates, cutlery and cups and add decorations or guest names to these.

And if you're having a themed party, the cloth can be decorated to match – maybe lots of spooky pictures for a Halloween party or eggs and chicks for an Easter lunch. It's up to you and your creative genius.

Best of all, you can leave pots of pens or crayons on the table for your guests to add more decorations.

Tip: You can use a glue stick to secure down the middle flap of your cloth if you want a neater finish.

Create a jellyfish in a bottle

Jellyfish make great pets. Not the real ones of course – they have a tendency to sting and they're rubbish at playing fetch. However, make your own and you'll find they're terribly well behaved and really quite cute.

First, you'll need a clear plastic bag. Cut this open along one side and the base so you have a flat sheet. Next, cut a piece out about 30cm x 30cm. Put two googly eyes in the centre and then gather the plastic sheet in around these so they are sitting in a little balloon shape about 3cm tall.

Now, tie the base of this with a piece of white thread. Make a knot, but not too tight as you will still need a little hole at the bottom of the balloon for filling with water.

Take your scissors and cut the dangling plastic so they form about eight 2cm wide strips. Remove any extra plastic by cutting it off about 1cm under the balloon.

Now, take your eight strips and start to cut them into thinner strips to form the tentacles. Try to make no tentacles longer than about 10cm and cut some shorter too for a bit of variety.

When you've finished, spread out the tentacles and hold the jellyfish upside down until you find the opening at the bottom of the head. Hold this under a flowing tap to fill it with water.

Fill your bottle nearly to the top with water and add some blue food colouring (if you want it to to look like the ocean) or another colour. While trying not to lose water from the jellyfish, push it into the bottle – you can use the handle of a wooden spoon or a lollipop stick to help if you need. When it's in, put on the lid and you can start tipping the bottle up and down and from side to side to watch your jellyfish swim.

YOU WILL NEED: CLEAR PLASTIC BAG, SCISSORS, GOOGLY EYES, WHITE THREAD, 1 LITRE BOTTLE, WATER, BLUE FOOD COLOURING (OPTIONAL)

Play wink murder

YOU WILL NEED: 5 OR MORE PLAYERS, PAPER, PEN OR PENCIL, CONTAINER, DREADFUL ACTING

If you believe a wink is a friendly or even cheeky gesture, then think again. In this game it will result in blood-curdling screams, accusations of murder and some pretty dreadful acting.

You need at least five people to play this game and ideally about ten or more. This means it's good at parties, or to liven up boring family gatherings where everyone just sits around asking you how school's going.

First, you'll need to decide on the murderer. Have the same number of folded pieces of paper as there are players. Mark one with a cross and leave the others blank. Next, everyone draws a piece of paper at random out of a hat or other container. The person with the cross will be the murderer but can't tell anyone their guilty secret.

Now, the game begins. The murderer has to try to kill off other players by winking at them. This does seem like a remarkably easy way to commit murder but the trick is not to let any of the other players see you do it. This isn't going to be simple as you will all be sitting in a circle or around a table together.

If a player is winked at, they must count to five before letting out a chilling scream or collapsing to the floor in a dramatic manner.

If any player thinks they know who the murderer is they can point to them and say, in a suitably theatrical fashion 'I accuse you of murder, you villainous rogue', or something slightly less flamboyant. If they guess correctly, they win. But if they have the wrong person they cannot guess again and must simply wait for the murderer to attack. Oh, and corpses can't accuse anyone (in case you were wondering).

If all but one innocent person is left 'alive' then the murderer is declared the winner.

The murderer can try to hide their true identity by joining in with the guessing.

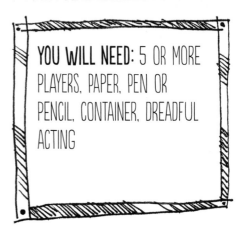

Tip: You can play a version where another of the pieces of paper has a circle on it and whoever gets this is the detective. Only this person can guess the murderer and they have just two chances to get it right.

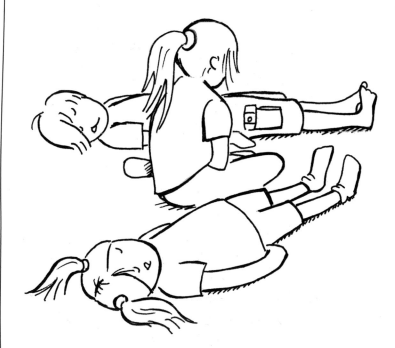

Give your room a view

Ever wish your bedroom had a better view? Well, perhaps it's time you did something about it. Grown-ups tend to complain if you try to sell their home and relocate, so it's best to use your artistic skills instead.

First, decide what you would like to see: rolling countryside, a big city, an alien planet. You could just paint a picture. But if you want the view to look really convincing (well, okay, not if it's an alien planet) then it helps to add perspective.

Perspective means a picture looks more realistic because things in the distance appear smaller – just like in real life.

To do this, take a ruler and draw a pencil line across the middle of your paper or a little higher to make the 'horizon line'. Somewhere along this line, add a dot – the vanishing point (where anything in your picture will be so small it'll have vanished from view).

Now, use your ruler to draw in some features. For example, if you want to add a road, place one end of the ruler on the vanishing point and the other where you want the outer edge of the road to end and draw in the line. Do the same for the other side and the central markings. You could add a fence or hedge by the side of the road using the same method or even a row of buildings. When you have drawn your main features in pencil you can complete them in paint.

To make the window frame use the same size of paper and lightly mark a line all around the edge 2.5cm deep. Fold the paper in half both ways to mark a cross shape – this is where the centre of your window bars will be. Draw a pencil line 1cm from either side of these and carefully cut a slit in the centre of each of the four panes so you can get your scissors in to cut them out.

Glue this frame on top of your picture and stick it on a blank bit of bedroom wall. Suddenly, you will have a far more interesting view to enjoy – and possibly alien invasions to worry about.

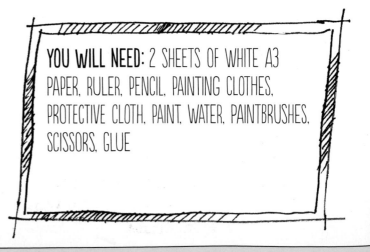

YOU WILL NEED: 2 SHEETS OF WHITE A3 PAPER, RULER, PENCIL, PAINTING CLOTHES, PROTECTIVE CLOTH, PAINT, WATER, PAINTBRUSHES, SCISSORS, GLUE

Tip: You can add a 3D effect by shading the bottom and sides of the window bars with light grey paint.

Tip: Include other details such as people, clouds or aliens. Just make sure the nearer they are to the vanishing point, the smaller they become.

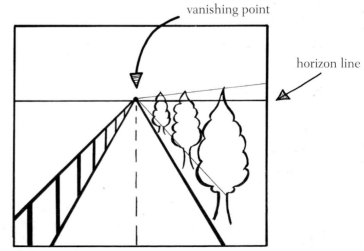

vanishing point

horizon line

Tip: Don't forget to add some interesting garden features – bridges, paths and even dinosaurs. That should liven up the place!

Tip: If you want to build a larger terrarium you could use an old fish tank with a lid.

Tip: You can add a 1.5cm layer of activated charcoal (available at pet shops) above the gravel – this keeps the terrarium smelling fresh.

Plant a terrarium

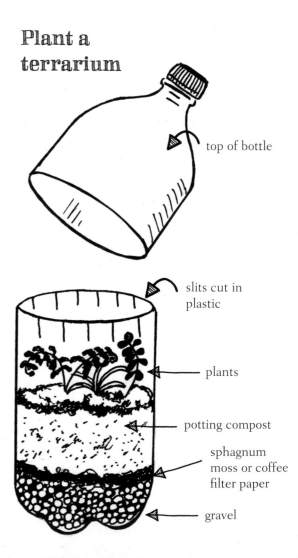

top of bottle

slits cut in plastic

plants

potting compost

sphagnum moss or coffee filter paper

gravel

Plant a terrarium

If it's too wet to play *in* the garden, why not play *with* a garden instead? It's just as much fun – and a lot quicker to weed and water.

First, take a clean, empty plastic bottle at least 2 litres in size and with uncoloured sides. Remove the lid, squash it flat in the middle and, using scissors, make a slit 20cm from the base. Keep cutting until you have separated the bottle into two pieces and then make several slits around the top edge of the bottle base, each about 2cm long.

Add a 3–4cm layer of gravel to the bottom of the bottle for excess water to drain into. Now, you'll need some potting compost – enough to fill half the space left. Put this in a bowl and pour in water, a little at a time, until you can shape the wet potting compost into a ball, but not so much that the ball drips water. Now, place the compost in the terrarium. You could add a circle of coffee filter paper or some sphagnum moss first to stop the compost getting mixed up with the layer below.

It's time now to plant. You need to have plants that can take the moist atmosphere of the terrarium. Mosses and lichens are a great start and can also add a lawn-like feel to your mini garden. Try tiny ferns, baby spider plants and African violets – just make sure nothing you plant will grow too large.

When you're happy with your garden, put the top section of the bottle (with its lid on) over the garden – the slits in the side of the bottle garden base will help it fit. Now, sit the terrarium somewhere that's light but not in direct sunlight.

As plants 'breathe', they lose water through their leaves and this will gather on the sides of your terrarium and eventually fall back into the soil as the temperatures and light levels drop. If there's not enough water forming on the sides, you may need to add more or move your garden further from the light. If there's too much, leave the top off your terrarium to allow some to escape.

YOU WILL NEED: EMPTY PLASTIC BOTTLE WITH A LID (AT LEAST 2 LITRES), SCISSORS, RULER, GRAVEL, POTTING COMPOST, BOWL, WATER, COFFEE FILTER PAPER (OPTIONAL), SPHAGNUM MOSS (OPTIONAL), PLANTS, ACTIVATED CHARCOAL (OPTIONAL)

Try salt painting

Salt doesn't exactly make you think 'art'. After all, there aren't many pictures that you can imagine creating with just this ingredient – unless you want to paint a snowman, juggling with white marshmallows in the Arctic, of course.

Thankfully, we will be using some colour too, so you can stop worrying.

First of all, you need a piece of card – any colour you want. This technique works well on light or dark backgrounds.

Now, you need to paint a picture using the glue. If you have a fine dispenser at the top of your bottle you can simply squeeze out your masterpiece. But if not, use a small paintbrush and keep dipping it in the glue to create the scene. And remember, strong, simple shapes work well.

When you are happy with your composition, you need to coat it in table salt. Make sure you sprinkle plenty of this on and tilt it backwards and forwards to cover the top and sides of the glue. You can then tip it up onto some old newspaper and save the extra salt to use on another picture.

Now comes the WOW! moment. On a paint tray or in small pots, add a few drops of food colouring to a tablespoon of water. Dip a clean paintbrush into this mixture and touch it to a section of your painting. The colour will instantly be absorbed by the salt and start travelling along the crystals. Use different colours and keep touching them to the raised salt pattern until the whole picture is complete. Unless, of course, you're still stuck on doing that juggling snowman portrait, in which case, this is going to be a lot less fun.

YOU WILL NEED: THIN CARD, PVA GLUE, TABLE OR COOKING SALT, NEWSPAPER (TO PROTECT TABLE AND COLLECT SALT), PAINT TRAY OR SMALL POTS, FOOD COLOURING, WATER, PAINTBRUSH

Tip: As the salt dries it will flake away, which means these pictures won't keep for long, so why not take some photos to capture and preserve your artworks?

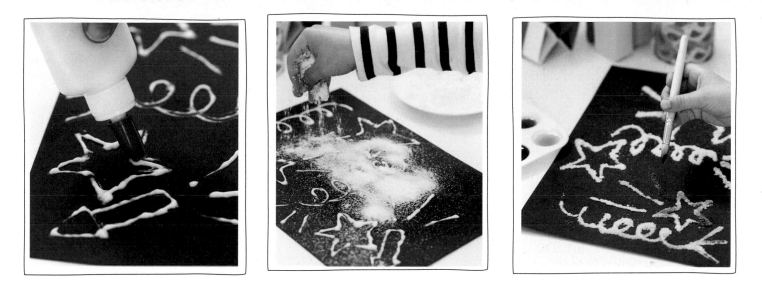

Tip: If you have watercolour paints you can use these instead
of the food colouring and water.

Cut out a shape from the front cover so you can see the contrast to the paper colour below.

Tie a knot in the end of an elastic band and use it as a pencil holder and notebook closer.

Folding your book

1.

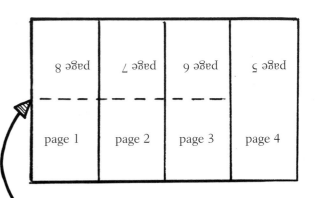

| page 8 | page 7 | page 6 | page 5 |
| page 1 | page 2 | page 3 | page 4 |

Cut along dotted line.

2.

Fold along the line between pages 4 and 5, then concertina fold the other pages.

3.

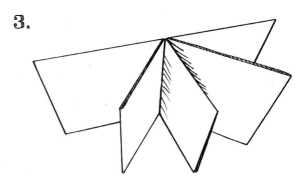

Glue together the three pairs of pages.

Fold a mini book

'So, what are you going to do this afternoon?'

'Well, I thought I might write a book.'

This is a brilliant way to sound super impressive. But when you've created your book from a single sheet of A4 it's a lot easier to fill those pages. In fact, why didn't I think of that? That could have saved me a lot of time.

First, you'll need to take your sheet and fold it in half lengthways, open it up and this time fold it in half in the other direction. Unfold and then, taking these same sides fold them in again but this time take each one only to the middle line. When you unfold again you will be left with eight rectangles marked out in creases.

Cut the longest line carefully three quarters of the way up and fold the paper at this remaining intact middle line. Now, concertina fold the other sheets so they lie flat – you'll need to do one side first, then turn over to complete the other.

Glue together three pairs of pages starting with the middle pair attached by the central fold, and then the pairs each side of this. You should be left with three double-thickness pages and a single thickness page at the front and back.

Add glue to the outside for the front sheet and lay this on your card, lining up the edges. Now, cut along the card where the top edge of the book lies. Put more glue on the outside of the back page of the book and bend the whole book over so this glued section is stuck to the other side of the card cover. Finally, cut along the card to complete the side and top of the book cover.

You now have the perfect book for taking orders in a café (see pages 78–79), creating passports for racing around the world (see pages 100–101), making workbooks for a school (see pages 42–43), constructing a mini photo album or writing a very short, bestselling novel.

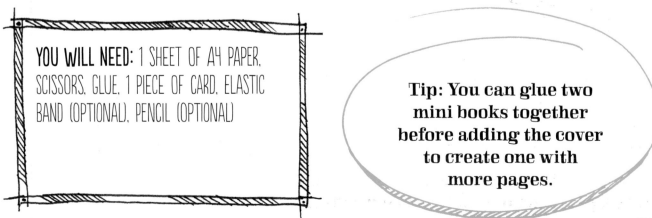

YOU WILL NEED: 1 SHEET OF A4 PAPER, SCISSORS, GLUE, 1 PIECE OF CARD, ELASTIC BAND (OPTIONAL), PENCIL (OPTIONAL)

Tip: You can glue two mini books together before adding the cover to create one with more pages.

Make string block prints

As the name suggests, you usually need blocks of wood for this kind of printing. Strangely, not many homes have a 'wood block cupboard' these days and, as I'm pretty sure your parents aren't going to give you a saw to cut your own, we're going to need to make the block.

Thankfully, it's an easy job.

All you need is some corrugated cardboard from an old box. Ideally, you'll have enough to mark and cut out five to six squares measuring 8cm x 8cm. Now, paste the top of one with PVA glue, place another over the top and keep doing this until you have a stack. Place a heavy book over these and leave them for at least half an hour to dry.

Complete your cardboard block by wrapping around it with the end of some string. Tie this tightly and then keep wrapping the string to form a random pattern before tying off the end the same side as the initial knot – this will be the 'non-printing' side.

If you place some paint on a flat dish or container so it covers the surface you can now dip in your string block and then press this down on a piece of paper. It's a good idea to experiment on some old newspaper first to make sure you are applying the right amount of paint each time.

When you are confident, you can start printing. It's very effective if you make prints next to each other each time but turn the block sideways every other print for a more interesting pattern. You can also experiment with alternating colours of paint or simply add a second 'highlight' colour by coating some pieces of the string with a paintbrush before printing.

You can also stick on shapes or swirls of string to a block and leave it to dry for another style of printing. And, of course, you could make some other blocks bigger or smaller by cutting different card sizes. In fact, at this rate, you will need a 'block printing cupboard' after all (but I'm still not letting you near a saw, so don't get any ideas).

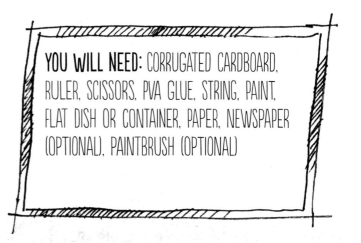

YOU WILL NEED: CORRUGATED CARDBOARD, RULER, SCISSORS, PVA GLUE, STRING, PAINT, FLAT DISH OR CONTAINER, PAPER, NEWSPAPER (OPTIONAL), PAINTBRUSH (OPTIONAL)

Tip: This is a quick way to cover a large sheet that you can then use as wrapping paper.

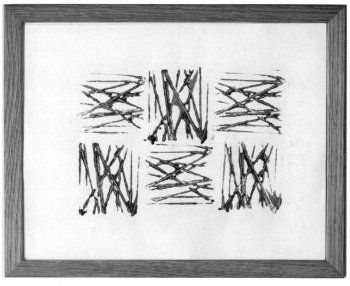

Tip: The block prints can make a very effective work of art, too.

Master 3D drawing

So, okay, 'master' might be going a bit far, but you will at least be able to create incredibly cool drawings with a 3D effect. 'Mastering' the entire range of 3D artistic skills – well, you can always do that next week.

First, take a sheet of white paper and place your hand and wrist across it. Using a pencil, trace this shape as carefully as possible, but don't press down too hard because you'll need to rub these lines out at the end.

Now, take a thick felt-tip pen and start drawing a line from one side of the paper. When you come to the outline of your wrist or arm, stop your pen and add in a curve that runs from one side of the outline to the other – as though you were drawing a small hill. When you reach the other side, again stop the pen and carry on in a straight line to the end of the paper.

Do this whenever you come across an outline. If it's the fingers, you'll need to draw the curve from one side of each finger to the other and put

in a straight line before adding another hill over the next finger.

You can either draw your felt-tip lines quite closely together or else do them every couple of centimetres to get the basic shape and infill with other lines afterwards.

For a more solid look, you could add black lines and then colour in the gaps between.

Whichever method you choose, once you have added enough lines and colour you will be able to see the finished effect of a hand apparently rising out of the drawing.

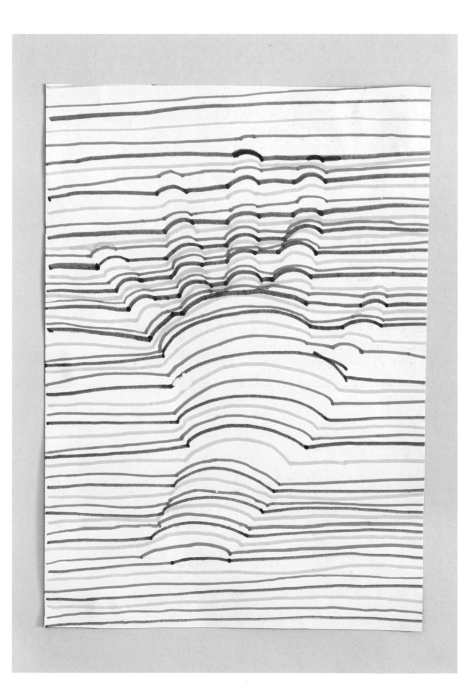

Tip: You can try out this technique with strong shapes like hearts or stars, or perhaps even your initials or name.

Play sticky note scramble

This is part treasure hunt, part race, and all mayhem. It's also the perfect use for sticky notes (if you haven't got through them all making flipbooks – see pages 86–87).

To begin, you need someone to think of objects or features that can be found around the house. They need to write one on each sticky note and enough to have 20 altogether – making ten per team or player. You can make it clear which are for which teams by using different coloured sticky notes or a different coloured pen.

The more precise the writer is, the better. So, instead of just putting 'door' they could note down 'downstairs toilet door' and instead of 'clock', how about 'pink alarm clock' (provided you have such a thing in the house, otherwise this game will be very frustrating).

Now, while players remain in one room, the game maker will go around the house deliberately mislabelling items until all the notes are used up. On 'Go' each player or team has to find their sticky notes and put them on the right object. To make it harder, the rule is you can only be holding one sticky note at a time and the winner is the first person or team to attach all their sticky notes to the correct objects.

Oh, and please don't go labelling people or pets – they tend to complain.

alarm clock

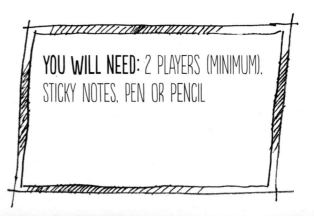

YOU WILL NEED: 2 PLAYERS (MINIMUM), STICKY NOTES, PEN OR PENCIL

fish
bowl

cookie
jar

toothbrush
holder

Tip: If you only have two players you can take it in turns to set out the sticky notes and the person who completes the task in the fastest time wins.

Make egg-shaped sculptures

This is the second greatest thing you can do with a water balloon. The first is fill it with ice cold water, put it down your brother's back and then pat it really hard. That is awesome. But this is close.

The first thing to do is blow up your water balloon to the size of a large egg – this can be easier if you use a balloon pump but otherwise just blow hard. Tie a knot in the end. The world is very clearly divided into those who can tie knots in balloons, and those who can't. If you can't, you'll need to locate a balloon tie-er – and fast!

Make your sticking mixture by adding a big dollop of PVA glue to a plastic bowl and stirring in a little bit of water to make a smooth paste – usually two parts glue to one part water.

Take one end of your wool, unwrap about 40cm and dip this into the glue mixture until it's well coated. Now, carefully begin to wrap it around the balloon. Make sure as you do this that the wool criss-crosses over itself at various points. When you've nearly finished this section, unravel another 40cm of wool, dip it in the mixture and carry on. When you are happy that the balloon is well covered, cut your wool, dip this last section in the glue mixture and wrap it round, tucking the final end underneath other wool strands.

Now, put it on a plastic plate to dry for a day. Yes, that's right, you have to wait a whole day. Still, it gives you plenty of time to put water balloons down people's backs in the meantime.

Finally, when the wool feels stiff, use a small pair of scissors to cut off the balloon end. As the balloon deflates, the sides might collapse a little. Don't panic! Just gently push them back into shape and leave it to dry for a little longer until you are left with a brilliant web-like wool egg.

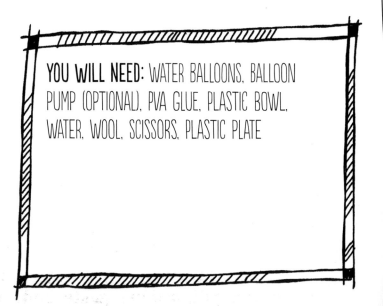

YOU WILL NEED: WATER BALLOONS, BALLOON PUMP (OPTIONAL), PVA GLUE, PLASTIC BOWL, WATER, WOOL, SCISSORS, PLASTIC PLATE

✎ **Tip: If you want a stronger egg – or a giant one made with a full-size balloon – use string dipped in a paste made of two parts flour and three parts water.**

Make a severed finger box

You know when grown-ups say ridiculous things like 'It's nicer to give presents than receive them'? – well, just for once, they may be onto something. In fact, you could try giving this special gift to your parents just to show them how right they are.

First, you'll need a small gift box. If you haven't got one to hand, don't worry, they are very easy to construct.

Take a piece of A4 card, fold it in half lengthways and then widthways, open it out and cut out two of the rectangles marked. Set the other two aside.

Take a ruler and mark some points 5.2cm in from the longest sides of one of the rectangles. Then, fold in the sides to meet these points and press down the folds.

Open it out and mark 5.2cm in from the top and bottom of the card and again fold and crease to these points before making cuts as shown in the diagram opposite.

You can now make a hole in the base of the box using the method on page 27. Finally, add glue or double-sided sticky tape to the flaps to stick the box together.

Use the second quarter of your A4 card to make the lid. Do this by following the same instructions as before but measure in 5cm from all sides so the lid is slightly larger, and don't cut a hole in this one.

Place some cotton wool in the base of your box, push your index finger through the hole, bend it over and dollop some tomato ketchup or red food colouring near your knuckle so it looks like it has been bleeding.

All you need to do now is place the top on your box and offer your 'gift' to someone 'special'.

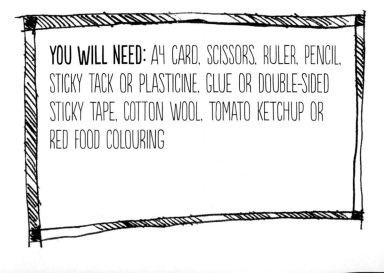

YOU WILL NEED: A4 CARD, SCISSORS, RULER, PENCIL, STICKY TACK OR PLASTICINE, GLUE OR DOUBLE-SIDED STICKY TAPE, COTTON WOOL, TOMATO KETCHUP OR RED FOOD COLOURING

Make the box

1.
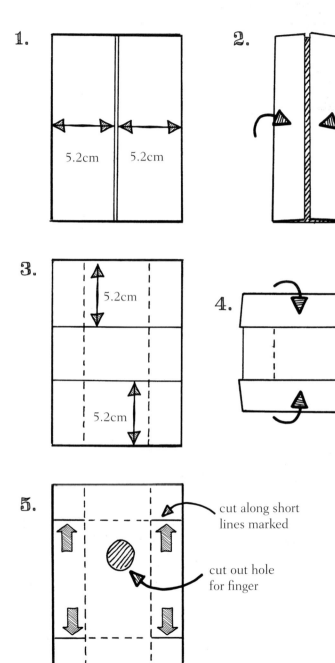

5.2cm   5.2cm

2.

3.

5.2cm

5.2cm

4.

5.

cut along short
lines marked

cut out hole
for finger

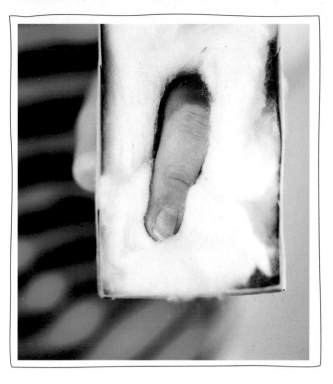

**Tip: For added authenticity, why not
add some talc or white make-up to your
finger so it looks less 'alive'.**

Catapult a paper plane

Tip: You can curl the end tips of your plane to alter its movement: curling both up will make it climb; curling both down will make it dive.

There are many different ways of folding and launching a paper plane but let's be clear about this – my way is the BEST.* Good. I'm glad we've got that straight.

You'll need to start with an A4 sheet of paper. Fold this lengthways, then crease and unfold so you have a line down the middle. Take the top right corner and fold it down to where the top edge meets the centre line. Do the same with the top left corner to form a triangle. Fold the triangle over so the point sits on the centre line.

Now, take the top left and right corners and fold them over so they meet about two thirds of the way down the triangle and then fold the tip of the triangle back up to hold these ends in place.

Bend the plane back on itself along the centre line so the wings are touching. Then, take a wing at a time and fold it downwards at the point where the top triangle begins and so the fold line is parallel to the centre line.

Hold together the undercarriage of your plane and place a piece of sticky tape either side, just behind the front section for reinforcement. Hole punch through this and thread an elastic band through the hole and then through itself and tighten.

You are now ready for launch. Of course, you could just throw the plane. But to give it real power place the elastic band over your thumb, pull the plane back towards you and when you're ready to launch, let go.

* Probably

Make a paper plane

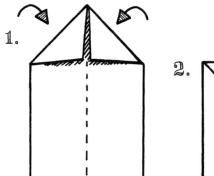

1.

2.

3.

4.

5.

fold plane back
on itself along
centreline
so wings are
touching

6.

punch hole

7.

Set up a juice bar

If you've raced around the world (see pages 100–101), played hands-free ping-pong (see pages 46–47) completed an obstacle course (see pages 154–155) or stomped some balloons (see pages 18–19) you're probably feeling a little bit thirsty right now. The perfect time to set up a juice bar.

You can experiment with different mixes and flavours but here are a few recipe ideas to get you started.

Fruit punch (enough for 2–3 servings)

In a jug, mix together 150ml cranberry juice, 150ml pineapple juice, 150ml ginger ale and a couple of drops of almond extract. Add ice to the glasses and pour to serve.

Coloured ice drinks

Fill an ice-cube tray with different fruit juices such as orange, cranberry and apple, and freeze it overnight. The next day you can press these out into a bowl, half-fill glasses with lemonade and then drop in a mix of colourful fruity ice cubes.

Apple Julep (enough for 2–3 servings)

Add 200ml apple juice, 50ml orange juice, 50ml pineapple juice and a squeeze of lemon to a jug. Stir well and pour into glasses filled with lots of ice and add a sprig of mint to the top as a garnish.

If these drinks are for a very special occasion, you could even add frosting and decorations around the rim of your glasses. To do this, just put a small amount of golden syrup in a cup and use a pastry brush or your very clean finger to add a thin layer of it around the top outside edge of each glass. You can now dust this with caster sugar or cover it with sprinkles.

If grown-ups start to get worried at the talk of syrup, sugar and sprinkles, remind them that this is just for show. Obviously, you will be drinking through a straw and will not be tempted, even for a minute, to lick the edge of the glass. And if they believe that...

Tip: For added glamour you can put colourful, curly straws in the drinks and make your own little decorative umbrellas from paper and cocktail sticks.

Roll paper beads

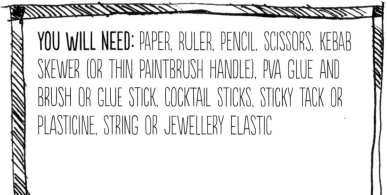

Who needs gold, silver or diamonds? It's perfectly possibly to make gorgeous jewellery from a few pieces of paper. It also requires a lot less pocket money and fewer security guards, which is never a bad thing.

First, take a sheet of paper and measure 1.5cm in from the bottom and mark off every 3cm. Do the same at the top, but just mark the 3cm intervals. Join these marks together so you form a series of long, thin triangles which you can cut out (throwing away the two partial shapes at either end). You can draw the triangles on in either direction – just remember, the longer the shape the larger the bead will be at the centre.

Take a kebab skewer and begin to tightly roll the paper onto it, starting at the widest end. When you are 1–2cm up the paper, add a strip of glue and keep rolling. Keep adding glue at intervals until you get to the last 3–4cm. Here, add a thin layer of glue to the rest of the paper and complete the roll. Slip your 'bead' off the kebab stick and place it to dry on a cocktail stick stuck upright in a lump of sticky tack or plasticine.

You can give the finished beads a coat of watered-down PVA glue. Do this about four times, allowing the glue to dry in between and the beads will be more water-resistant and shiny. You can thread them onto string or jewellery elastic to form bracelets and necklaces.

You can use all sorts of different paper to make your beads, such as old magazines, wrapping paper or newspaper. Just remember that very thin paper may rip more easily and thicker paper is harder to roll. And avoid gold leaf paper – otherwise we're back with the pocket money/security guard problem again.

Tip: If you don't have a skewer you could use a thin paintbrush handle or even a pencil or pen for the bead roller.

Roll a paper bead

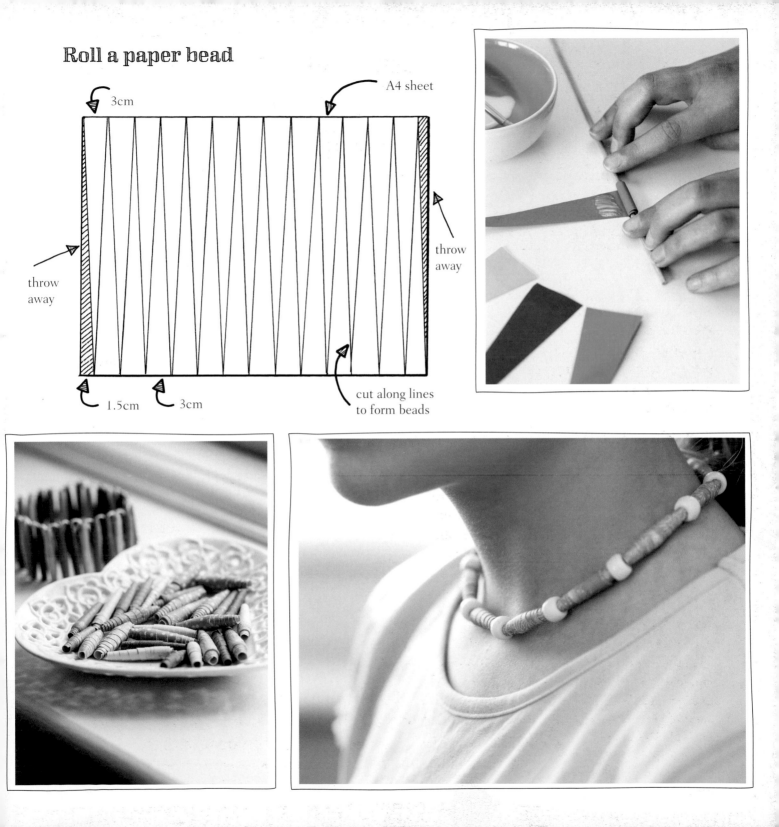

3cm

A4 sheet

throw away

throw away

throw away

1.5cm   3cm

cut along lines to form beads

Have a backwards day

Sadly, this activity will not actually let you control time – otherwise we'd just be running the summer holidays forwards and backwards for months on end. However, it is a way to make an otherwise ordinary day a bit more interesting.

You'll probably want to get your parents on board first, not least because they'll just think you've gone a bit loopy otherwise. And it might be worth planning things out in advance – especially mealtimes.

And apart from that, it's just about turning as much of the day on its head as you can.

You can start by wishing everyone goodnight, skulking around in your pyjamas for a couple of hours with all the curtains drawn and having bedtime stories with milk and cookies. You'll need to get dressed in time to sit down for dinner in the morning but you should feel free to put your clothes on back to front and don't forget to eat dessert first. Oh, and if you want to sit under the table to eat that's fine by me (what your parents think is another matter).

As far as activities go, you could play seek and hide (aka Sardines), backwards running races, trying to lose, rather than win, any game, or reading this book backward (hey, look at that, the first idea is then a backwards day!)

By the evening you'll be getting ready for breakfast before saying good morning to everyone and heading back to bed.

Oh, and don't forget you can rename yourself for the day by saying your name backwards – unless you're called Ava, Hannah, Otto or Bob, in which case that's just cheating.

Tip: If you really want a mixed-up day, you can always try swapping roles with your parents. WARNING – being a grown-up really isn't as much fun as you think.

Resources

UK

Argos
Online or high street shops good for items such as torches, timers, ping pong balls and fairy lights.
www.argos.co.uk
0845 6403030

Baker Ross
Huge range of craft accessories including paper, card, paints and brushes, sticky tapes, scissors, glue, beads, lollipop sticks, tracing paper, envelopes, string, googly eyes, ribbon, foam and felt sheets, mirror card, pipecleaners, and marker pens.
www.bakerross.co.uk
0844 576 8922

B&Q
Wide selection of supplies including compost, plant pots, seeds, twine, and sand. Also good for paint and varnish, duct tape, masking tape and sandpaper.
www.diy.com
0845 609 6688

Dunelm Mill
Useful for fabric, oilcloths, zips, needles and thread, wool as well as many household items such as tea lights and much more.
www.dunelm-mill.com
0845 1656565

Garden centres
There are various garden centres across the country and you should find your local one is a good all year round source of gardening supplies, seeds and plants. You can find local centres by searching The Garden Centre Association
www.gca.org.uk
0118 930 8918

John Lewis
Department store and online shop which supplies fabric and sewing accessories such as pinking shears as well as general household items.
www.johnlewis.com
03456 049 049

Lakeland
Useful for household supplies such as citric acid, graters, wooden spoons and cupcake moulds.
www.lakeland.co.uk
01539 488100

Pharmacies
Often good places to find essential oils, citric acid and antacid tablets.
Find your local one at http://www.pharmacyregulation.org/registers/pharmacy
0203 713 8000

Ryman
Good for stationary items including graph paper, tracing paper, card, glue etc as well as playing cards.
www.ryman.co.uk
0800 801901

Wilko
Great source of good value household items such as jugs, bowls, spray bottles, wooden spoons, cupcake moulds, hair grips and timers. Also good for craft items such as double sided sticky tape, balloons, duct tape, masking tape, sandpaper, varnish and card as well as garden supplies in season.
www.wilko.com
08456 080807

Australia

Big W
Craft and game supplies.
www.bigw.com.au
038831 9777

Bunnings Warehouse
Garden supplies and household items from bamboo canes to tea lights.
www.bunnings.com.au
1300 244 999

Kmart
Home, game and garden supplies.
www.kmart.com.au
1800 124 125

Categories

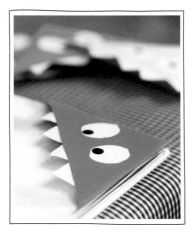

Perfect for presents

Great games

Quick projects

Good for younger children (age 3–7)

Play balloon stomp (**p.18**)

Grow an eggcup micro garden (**p.20**)

Make a play dough ice-cream parlour (**p.22**)

Wrap the mummy (**p.24**)

Hold a dress-up race (**p.34**)

Conjure up ice cream in a bag (**p.36**)

Set up a school (**p.42**)

Compete in hands-free ping pong (**p.46**)

Watch water walk (**p.51**)

Craft stained glass lanterns (**p.68**)

Learn to paper patchwork and decoupage (**p.73**)

Set up a café (**p.78**)

Have an indoor snowball fight (**p.82**)

See how low you can go (**p.90**)

Hunt the thingy (**p.94**)

Make green gloop (**p.98**)

Make a heart garland (**p.114**)

Grow a garden from scraps (**p.119**)

Hold a butter-making race (**p.128**)

Make corner bookmarks (**p.133**)

Play flap the fish (**p.142**)

Set up an indoor obstacle course (**p.154**)

Craft with papier mâché (**p.172**)

Try salt painting (**p.190**)

Good for older children (age 7+)

Concoct bath bombs (**p.13**)

Create crossword cards (**p.14**)

Weave a multi-braided bracelet (**p.28**)

Pour colour-changing drinks (**p.31**)

Hold a junk fashion show (**p.32**)

Teach yourself a card game (**p.40**)

Remodel your bedroom (**p.44**)

Construct a card tower (**p.56**)

Play patience (**p.60**)

Take and lift fingerprints (**p.66**)

Create a kaleidoscope (**p.84**)

Set up a spa (**p.88**)

Construct a no-sew shoulder bag (**p.92**)

Design your own board game (**p.124**)

Make fifteens (**p.136**)

Prepare a fruity melon bowl (**p.139**)

Construct a lava lamp (**p.146**)

Prepare fresh strawberry tiramisu (**p.148**)

Build a solar system mobile (**p.158**)

Make a no-sew pencil case (**p.162**)

Play shadow charades (**p.164**)

Run your own library (**p.174**)

Erupt a volcano (**p.176**)

Play wink murder (**p.184**)

Roll paper beads (**p.208**)

Have a backwards day (**p.210**)

Best for cooks

Mix up a dip fest (**p.16**)

Conjure up ice cream in a bag (**p.36**)

Freeze fruity ice lollies (**p.110**)

Hold a butter-making race (**p.128**)

Make fifteens (**p.136**)

Prepare a fruity melon bowl (**p.139**)

Prepare fresh strawberry tiramisu
  (**p.148**)

Create pinwheel sandwiches (**p.162**)

Make rainbow fruit kebabs (**p.168**)

Set up a juice bar (**p.206**)

Best for scientists

Pour colour-changing drinks (**p.31**)

Conjure up ice cream in a bag (**p.36**)

Watch water walk (**p.51**)

Take and lift fingerprints (**p.66**)

Make green gloop (**p.98**)

Draw optical illusions (**p.116**)

Construct a lava lamp (**p.146**)

Launch a Magnus glider (**p.156**)

Build a solar system mobile (**p.158**)

Erupt a volcano (**p.176**)

Best for tricksters

Pour colour-changing drinks (**p.31**)

Become a mind reader (**p.104**)

Booby trap your bedroom (**p.141**)

Learn a magic trick (**p.178**)

Make a severed finger box (**p.202**)

BANG!!

Wonders from wool

Craft pom-poms (p.27)
Weave a multi-braided bracelet (p.28)
Learn to finger knit (p.58)
Wrap a yarn tin vase (p.134)
Make egg-shaped sculptures (p.200)

Best for gardeners

Grow an eggcup micro garden (p.20)
Grow a garden from scraps (p.119)
Plant a terrarium (p.189)

No-mess activities

Play 'Who am I?' (p.10)
Teach yourself a card game (p.40)
Learn some dice games (p.48)
Construct a card tower (p.56)
Make a flipbook (p.87)
Hunt the thingy (p.94)
Become a mind reader (p.104)
Draw optical illusions (p.116)
Play patience (p.172)
Play wink murder (p.184)
Catapult a paper plane (p.204)

Best for glamour

Concoct bath bombs (p.13)

Weave a multi-braided bracelet (p.28)

Hold a junk fashion show (p.32)

Remodel your bedroom (p.44)

Try out hairstyles (p.70)

Set up a spa (p.88)

Construct a no-sew shoulder bag (p.92)

Make a heart garland (p.114)

Best for artists

Hold a junk fashion show (p.32)

Fashion some spoon dolls (p.62)

Mix bath paints (p.74)

Make a flipbook (p.87)

Draw optical illusions (p.116)

Create silhouette portraits (p.167)

Decorate a tablecloth (p.180)

Give your room a view (p.186)

Try salt painting (p.190)

Make string block prints (p.194)

Master 3D drawing (p.196)

Make egg-shaped sculptures (p.200)

Homemade toys and games

Bigger projects

Index

Acknowledgements

Thank you to everyone at Kyle Books – especially my editor, Tara O'Sullivan, for making the whole process so smooth, and Kyle Cathie herself for supporting '101 Things' from the start. Also, to my agent Martine Carter for her wise counsel and ability to make things happen.

And for transforming this book into a thing of beauty I must thank Rachel Warne, a photographer extraordinaire, as well as Louise Leffler for another gorgeous book design and Sarah Leuzzi, whose illustrations are never less than genius.

My gratitude also goes to Gemma and Graham Bassett and Simon Smith, who not only allowed us to use their beautiful homes for photo shoots but didn't flinch when we littered those houses with children wielding glue sticks and glitter and the occasional exploding volcano.

Those children themselves have brought this book to life, so thank you to my top models: Joe, Tia, Evie S, Lana, Yulia, Darcy, Erin, Naomi, Mason, Rosie, Evie A and Lois.

And finally, my biggest thanks go to my family: to my mother Rosemary and my mother-in-law Hilary for their hands-on help and support, to my husband Reuben (the best move I ever made), and to Ava, Oscar and Archie who are a constant source of inspiration, amusement and pride. I love you all.